MONASTERY JOURNEY TO
Christmas

BROTHER VICTOR-ANTOINE
D'AVILA-LATOURRETTE

Liguori
LIGUORI, MISSOURI

Imprimi Potest:
Harry Grile, CSsR, Provincial
Denver Province, The Redemptorists

Published by Liguori Publications
Liguori, Missouri 63057

To order, call 800-325-9521, or visit liguori.org

Library of Congress Cataloging-in-Publication Data

D'Avila-Latourrette, Victor-Antoine.
   A monastery journey to Christmas / Victor-Antoine D'Avila-Latourrette.—1st ed.
   p. cm.
   ISBN 978-0-7648-2081-6
   1. Advent—Meditations. 2. Christmas—Meditations. I. Title.
   BV40.D38 2011
   242'.33—dc23

                                                          2011026911

Liguori Publications, a nonprofit corporation, is an apostolate of the Redemptorists. To learn more about the Redemptorists, visit Redemptorists.com.

Printed in the United States of America
15 14 13 12 11 / 5 4 3 2 1
First Edition

CONTENTS

INTRODUCTION

Maranatha!
Come, Lord Jesus!
O come, O come, Emmanuel!

The Advent and Christmas seasons are the liturgical times dedicated exclusively to reliving the mystery of the Incarnation. Advent, as we know, is a time of quiet waiting, of deep longing and intense praying, while we eagerly prepare for the Lord's arrival. During this blessed period of preparation, full of wonder and joyful anticipation, the Christian takes time out of a usually busy schedule to ponder in the depths of his or her heart the *Mirabilia Dei*, that is, the wonderful works of God as manifested in the mystery of his Son's Incarnation. During our moments of quiet prayer, our faith seems to increase, and we are deeply moved by hope and love to await in joyful expectancy the Savior's imminent coming. Indeed, we are filled with an immense desire for his presence as we look forward to welcoming him into the depths of our hearts.

This monastic book follows day-by-day the traditional rhythm of the Advent/Christmas journey as it takes place in a particular monastery, a place as small and tiny as Bethlehem itself.

The Advent journey, or "Advent fast" as others call it, usually begins around mid-November, exactly forty days before Christmas Day. In the early Church (and as continues to be the norm in the Eastern churches today) the Advent/Christmas fast consisted of a period of forty days' preparation, similar to the Lenten/Easter fast. During these forty days, we journey through the Advent desert like the Israelites of old, guided by the Spirit of God, by his word, and instructed by the prophets. Like all journeys and pilgrimages, and comparable to that of Lent, the Advent/Christmas journey has its ups and downs; therefore we often pray to the Holy Spirit for enlightenment, for patience, and for spiritual support.

As we journey along and eventually reach the summit—Christmas Day—we experience a certain sense of fullness as we behold our God under the appearances of a tiny baby, surrounded by angels, animals, shepherds, and of course by his earthly parents, our Lady and the good Saint Joseph. Though it reaches its plenitude at Christmas, the journey continues onward to Epiphany and Theophany, where the Lord manifests himself to the gentiles and to the whole world. Finally, forty days after Christmas, the journey reaches its completion on February 2, Candlemas Day, the feast of the Presentation of the Lord.

This book, as it depicts the monastic path to Christmas, is divided into small, often short chapters or reflections for each day of the journey. They follow the sequence of days and the calendar of both the Eastern and Western churches. In doing this, we find ourselves enriched by the logical complementariness of both traditions; for after all, it is the one and the same Messiah we await, the one and the same Lord Jesus Christ we both adore and worship. The short reflections, based usually on a liturgical text, feast, custom, or family Advent/Christmas tradition, allow the reader to connect and discover both new and ancient ways for keeping holy the celebration of the Lord's birth. And they provide the spiritual means for enjoying in depth the beauty of the Christmas festivities. Some reflections end with Latin phrases or sentences. If you would like to see translations, please go to pages 207 and 208. This book is all about Advent, Christmas, Epiphany, Theophany, and Candlemas, all about places such as Nazareth, Bethlehem, the river Jordan, the holy city of Jerusalem—and ultimately all about a preparatory journey toward the unfolding of the mystery to be revealed: God incarnate, Christ the Lord!

I owe a debt of gratitude to two Vassar alumni, Michael Centore and Sarah Harshman, graduates in 2002 and 2011, respectively, who helped with some of the typing and formatting of the manuscript. Also my deep thanks to Luis Medina and Pamela Brown of Liguori Publications for their warm collaboration in bringing this book to the public.

BROTHER VICTOR-ANTOINE
JUNE 24, 2011
SOLEMNITY AND NATIVITY OF SAINT JOHN THE BAPTIST,
PRECURSOR OF THE LORD

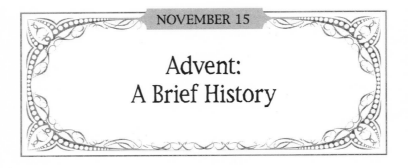

NOVEMBER 15

Advent:
A Brief History

Lead, kindly Light, amid the encircling gloom—Lead
  Thou me on!
The night is dark, and I am far from home—Lead
  Thou me on!
Keep thou my feet. I do not ask to see the distant
  scene, one step is enough for me.

BLESSED JOHN HENRY CARDINAL NEWMAN (1801–1890)

The season of Advent, containing a wealth of spiritual tradition and practices, has its origins in antiquity, in the early centuries of the Church. It is hard to pinpoint exactly the precise moment Advent was instituted as a liturgical season. In the Christian East, the season was conceived as a forty-day fasting period in preparation for the feast of the Nativity of the Lord. In this and many other ways, Advent was similar to the Lenten fast that leads to Easter. In the East, this time of preparation started around November 15, when Eastern Christians celebrated the feast of the Apostle Philip. Hence it is sometimes called "the Saint Philip fast."

Likewise in the West, it was the practice of the Church of France to have a similar penitential season leading ultimately to the celebrations of Christmas and Epiphany. It was the custom in France to start the fast on November 11, the feast of Saint Martin. For that reason, it was often referred to as "the Saint Martin fast." One of the earliest documents that comments on the concrete spiritual practices of this period is the second book in *Ten Books of Histories* by Saint Gregory of Tours, bishop of Tours, around 480 AD. Gregory relates in his books that the Christians in his diocese usually practiced three weekdays of fasting (Mondays, Wednesdays, and Fridays) in preparation for the Christmas/Epiphany/Theophany celebrations. A bit earlier, around 330 AD, the Church of Spain at the Council of Saragossa ordered a time of prayer and fasting before the feast of the Epiphany/Theophany that was similar to the practices observed in the Christian East. Around 581, a synod held in Macon, France, extended this Advent preparation to the rest of the diocese of France. From France, the Advent observance spread to England and the northern European countries. The fasting aspect was emphasized as an ascetical practice, and it ultimately led to the feast of the Epiphany/Theophany, which celebrated God's manifestation during Jesus' baptism in the Jordan.

The *Adventus Domini* (the coming of the Lord) observance arrived late in Rome. It was only adopted as such around the sixth or seventh centuries. It was the custom of the Roman Church to place emphasis on Christmas, the feast of the Nativity of the Lord. This was in contrast to the customs of the churches of the East and France, where emphasis was placed on the feasts of the Epiphany/Theophany. Pope Gregory the Great, a trained monk living under the Rule of Saint Benedict, developed the theme of the *Adventus Domini* in many of his homilies. He also established around the seventh century the Advent Roman rite style more or less as we know it today. For a while, there was a back-and-forth period of experimentation between the Roman practice and the one of the Church of France. At one point, the French churches accepted some of the improvements brought about by Pope Gregory. At the same time, Rome and the other Churches accepted the French Church's emphasis on the Second/final Coming of the Lord during the Advent liturgy. The theol-

ogy of the Lord's final coming in power and majesty was central to the Advent liturgical practice of the French Church, which coincided in part with the practice also found in the Eastern churches. According to present usage in the Western Church, Advent begins on the Sunday nearest to the feast of the Apostle Andrew (November 30). This is similar to the Eastern custom of starting Advent close to the feast of another Apostle, Saint Philip (November 15). In the Roman rite, the Advent season comprises about four weeks, or a minimum of four Sundays. The first Sunday of Advent may fall as early as November 27.

In both the churches of the East and the West, the Advent season or Advent fast is considered as an ascetical and prayerful spiritual journey in preparation for the solemn commemoration of the Lord's birth, and ultimately for his Second Coming in glory. In the Church of the East, Saint Gregory Nazianzen was the great proponent of the Advent/Christmas observances; thus he wrote beautiful, poignant homilies on those themes. The mystery of the Incarnation and the festival of the Lord's birth were at all times on his mind. In appearance, the Advent liturgical traditions from the East and the West may seem to differ in certain aspects and practices, but deep down I find they complement and complete each other in the one and common celebration of the Nativity and Theophany of our Lord and Savior.

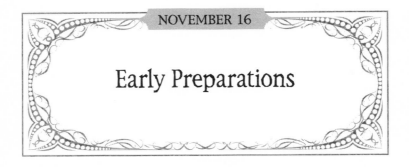

Early Preparations

All peoples of the earth,
All children of men,
Rich and poor alike, go out to meet him crying:
"Shepherd of Israel, hear us,
You who lead Joseph's race like a flock,
Tell us if you are the One."

MATINS RESPONSORY FOR ADVENT

reparations for the Advent and Christmas seasons start early in our monastery. Early in the autumn, we begin making preparations for our annual monastery Christmas craft fair, which takes place during the first week of Advent. Autumn is such a busy season here. We are plunged into multiple harvest activities: canning and freezing vegetables for our winter fare, gathering and splitting wood to sustain our three wood-burning stoves through the cold months ahead, storing hay bales in the barn for the sheep. Besides all these daily activities, the gardens are slowly being put to rest, and the last of the potted plants are being brought inside the greenhouse to save them for the next garden season.

While all these seasonal activities are taking place in the

monastery, we are also mindful that the time of the craft fair is quickly approaching and therefore we must hasten with preparations for the yearly sale. Principal among our preparations is the construction of the small Nativity scenes, or "crèches," as we love to call them in French. The word "crèche" is almost identical to the English word "crib," and in either language it is a word that warms the human heart intimately. Christmas abounds with multiple cultural traditions, as every country and people try to portray in their native crèche their own particular cultural depiction of the mystery of the Incarnation. Here

in the monastery, we try to remain attentive to these transcultural expressions as we build the physical settings for each crèche. The figurines or "santons" that compose each crèche come from many diverse countries. Thus, we cannot simply place them in just any form, setting, or arrangement. We must remain sensitive to the culture of origin and create the adequate type of setting. There, these lovely figures may feel at home. Jesus, through the mystery of his Incarnation, wishes to feel at home in each home and culture, for his message of salvation is for all humankind. He comes as a Savior to all.

During these late-fall days, in the silence and quiet of the monastery, we labor with steady intensity to make the crèches and other handicrafts for the Christmas fair. Our monastic silence provides a rich inspiration during our work. It allows us to be sensitive to the foreign, faraway cultures where some of the crèche figures have their origin. The pensive atmosphere also makes us aware of the natural products (wood, stone, hay, etc.) that are used in the fabrication of the scenes. These products are recycled materials, used again for a higher purpose. For this reason, they must be treated with care and respect. These early preparations are filled with the joy of anticipation, the sort of joy that culminates and finds its completion on Christmas Day. *"Iucundare, filia Sion, exsulta satis, filia Jerusalem."*

NOVEMBER 17

Advent Plans: Quiet Stillness

Seek the Lord while he may be found; call him while he is near. Alleluia.

ADVENT ANTIPHON

nterestingly, our Thanksgiving celebrations are barely approaching and people seem to be ready to jump right into the Christmas celebrations. The commercialization of the season in the media, in the stores, and in other such places is no help whatsoever in preparing for Christmas. For instead of focusing on Advent as a preparatory time, they distract us with their glitter, sights, and sounds, creating a false allure of celebration that is neither Christian nor real. The Scriptures tell us that there is a time and season for everything, for each particular event. There is a time of preparing for Christmas, and that is Advent, and then there is a time for Christmas itself. There is no doubt in my mind that the more serious we are about our personal Advent journey, the greater the joy we shall reap during our Christmas celebration.

It is a good practice to make concrete plans on how best to keep our Advent observance. Often, if no plans are made in advance, much of Advent goes unnoticed and wasted. Since Advent is basically a quiet time of waiting for the arrival of the Light at Christmas, it is good to start by trying to become more internally quiet during this rather brief season. It is also important to make a point to observe quiet time during the day for prayer, reading, reflection, or even just for a quiet stroll through the wonders of nature. If we are serious about integrating a quality quiet time into our daily routine, we shall discover the marvels it can work in our personal lives. Some of the quiet time can also be spent writing to those with whom we are close and with whom we

have not been in touch in a while. During our quiet time, we can also anticipate some early Christmas preparations, but without the rush or frantic obsession one observes on the last days just before December 25. Above all, we must make the most of these moments of stillness by remaining calm, silent, and spending quality time with the Lord. The words from one of the psalms counsel us: "Be still, and know that I am God." Monks always strive to preserve a more quiet recollected spirit during these lovely Advent days and thus enjoy the Lord's intimate company. There is no reason why others, in a monastery or elsewhere, could not do the same wherever they are. It is a question of resolving to do so and making the effort. The Holy Spirit shall do the rest. "*Veni, Sancte Spiritus.*"

NOVEMBER 18

Advent Waiting

*Be patient, therefore, brothers, until the coming of
the Lord. See how the farmer awaits the precious
fruit of the earth, being patient with it until it receives the early and the late rains. You too must be
patient. Make your hearts firm, because the coming
of the Lord is at hand.*

JAMES 5:7–8

Desires are nourished by delays.

ENGLISH PROVERB

Advent is primarily about waiting. It is about waiting
for the Lord to come. There is something special about
this particular type of waiting. First of all, waiting is a
spiritual attitude we cultivate deep within ourselves. We know
the Lord is coming, and therefore we desire and hasten his arrival by a patient attitude of waiting for him. We wait and wait
for the Lord. We become very conscious of the waiting. It is an
eager waiting, full of anticipation and wonder, for as the prophets of old, our companions on the road, we long to see his face.

The Lord, of course, is very much aware of this patient waiting, of this deep yearning for him, and he is ever ready to come

into our lives and fulfill our deepest desires. Advent waiting is always twofold. On our part, we await prayerfully, consciously, and anticipate his coming. On God's part, he is eager to arrive and find a warm dwelling place in our hearts. The greater our desire and patience in waiting for him, the fuller we shall be filled with his presence.

The early Christians, as the Apostle James reminds us, lived daily, steadily, waiting patiently for the Lord. Of course they thought this was going to be the Lord's final, triumphant coming and it was going to happen very soon, thus they wished to be ready

for it. Perhaps at one point they were a bit disappointed that it didn't occur according to their expectations. At the end, it didn't matter, for their eager waiting for him was rewarded by the Lord entering into their lives more fully and transforming every inch of their beings. Furthermore, many of them were blessed with a physical

vision of the Lord just before they underwent martyrdom. The Lord may not always act according to our expectations. After all, he tells us in the Scripture, "My thoughts are not your thoughts, nor are your ways my ways." Yet he never disappoints us.

If we learn to cultivate this inner attitude of waiting for him steadily, faithfully, not only during the blessed Advent days, but throughout the whole of our lives, we shall likewise be rewarded with the grace, joy, and warmth of his real presence in the innermost of our hearts. *Ecce, Salvator venit.*

The Prophets:
Our Guides on the Journey

Isaiah, as he kept watch by night, beheld the light that knows no evening, the light of your Manifestation, O Christ, which revealed your tender love for us. As he beheld the light he cried aloud: "Behold, a Virgin shall conceive and shall bear the Incarnate Word, and all those born on earth shall rejoice exceedingly."

BYZANTINE COMPLINE, FOREFEAST OF THE NATIVITY

The prophets, receiving the gift of prophecy from the same Word, foretold his coming in the flesh, which brought about the union and communion between God and man, ordained by the Father. From the beginning the word of God prophesied that God would be seen by men and would live among them on earth; he would speak with his own creation and be present to it, bringing it salvation and being visible to invisible.

FROM A TREATISE BY SAINT IRENAEUS

As we get older we tend to think more about our memories from the past than about our unpredictable future. I know I often do so, and many others do likewise. In the last couple of years I have found myself yearning more and more for the presence and lessons from the prophets. Their stark, austere presence has awakened something in me, especially during Advent. I often find myself hungering for the prophetic word. The prophets have become somehow so present, alive, and so real to me that I keep longing for icons of these individual prophets

in our chapel. I have a great desire, almost a need, to see them visually. I am quite aware it has grown in me a similar esteem for the prophets as the one I have for the four evangelists. I see more and more how well they complement one another. We do have an icon of a prophet in our chapel, that of the prophet Elijah, and it enhances a prayerful presence in our place of worship. How I wish our small chapel could also have the presence of Isaiah, Moses, Jeremiah, and especially King David. But if their icons are missing, we do have their prophetic words in the Scriptures to enlighten our faith and nourish our minds and hearts. Advent, somehow, is an evocative time to quietly listen to the prophets, God's messengers, and to take to heart their message.

Through the message from the prophets, God slowly began preparing the chosen moment in history when he would send his only Son, the "Anointed One," the Savior, into the world.

From the very beginning God had a plan, and in this plan there is a progression, a gradual revelation of the Messiah in the Old Testament. The prophets, the Lord's true servants, adapted themselves to it, sometimes painfully so, and gave their complete obedience to every aspect of the Lord's plan.

During these preparatory weeks before Christmas, we, too, are invited to ponder attentively God's plan and to listen to the prophetic words with the ears of our hearts, as Saint Benedict counsels us, letting the Lord unfold before our minds and eyes his eternal plan of salvation. We are invited not only to listen to the prophets but to go a step further and make our own their sentiments and message. Our world today longs as much for the Messiah, a Savior, as it did during the times of the prophets. Isaiah beautifully expresses humanity's deep longing for redemption, for a personal Savior: "Let justice descend, you heavens, like dew from above, like gentle rain let the clouds drop it down. Let the earth open and salvation bud forth; let righteousness spring up with them" (Isaiah 45:8)!

Guided by Isaiah, Jeremiah, Amos, Daniel, Micah and all the other ancient prophets, we are encouraged to walk our Advent journey along the path marked by these our wise and righteous fathers in the faith. With the prophets as our fellow companions and teachers, we should embark upon what the Gospels call the narrow way, learning profound wisdom from the prophetic words until we reach the summit of our Advent journey, Christmas Day, the moment when the glorious vision announced by the prophets becomes manifested to our eyes. On that day, in the words of the prophet Isaiah, we shall "shout with exultation, City of Zion, for great in your midst is the Holy One of Israel" (Isaiah 12:6).

NOVEMBER 20

The Lord's Forerunner

The figure of John the Baptist stands at the begin-
ning of Christian history...John proclaimed the
Jewish ideal of the kingdom of God, and he himself
soon became, within the tradition, the beginning of
its Gospel, announcing not only the coming of the
Christian Savior, but echoing its call to repentance
and conversion across the centuries. Even today his
is a voice in the wilderness, calling ever-new genera-
tions to answer the challenge posed by his person so
many centuries ago.

CARL KAZMIERSKI, *JOHN THE BAPTIST: PROPHET AND EVANGELIST*

All throughout Advent, we are led seriously by John the
precursor and by the prophets into the Advent desert
experience. In the desert, we hear John's solemn and
incontestable message: "Prepare the way of the Lord." His message becomes our primary Advent undertaking, our task at
hand, the only thing that really matters.

John the Baptist reminds us that Advent, a season of grace,
is a unique opportunity for an intimate interaction between the
Lord and us. It is certainly a time, aided by prayer and fasting,

to strengthen our own personal relationship with God. In the Advent desert, the Lord pours gratuitously his abundant graces into our hearts through his Holy Spirit, as he also demands our humble obedience and total cooperation with his plans. John's message to his disciples is very clear and appropriate, and it also applies to us today: We must take these Advent days seriously and humbly prepare our hearts for the Lord's coming. In the depth of the desert John's voice is heard, crying out aloud: "Prepare the way of the Lord." John knows from experience the

task at hand is not an easy one and thus he makes recourse to Isaiah's words to invite us "to level out the hills and the valleys"; that is, he urges us to remove from our lives all that is false, all those concrete obstacles that impede God from taking complete possession of our lives.

John's message, proclaimed once in the wasted landscape of the Judean desert, resounds with utmost clarity and with a contemporary tone today wherever Christians find themselves struggling to make a path for the Lord. John the Baptist's role comes into the scene at the tail end of centuries of messianic preparation preached by the prophets to the people of Israel. In the end, there is no longer need for other intermediaries; and it is to John, God's chosen one, upon whom falls the task of pointing the Messiah directly to the Jews: "Behold, the Lamb of God, who takes away the sin of the world." If we follow John's counsel, a counsel to change and repent, as we go along and penetrate with him into the remotest corners of the desert, we shall find there the Lord waiting patiently for us. In the aridity and nakedness of the desert, God is waiting to receive and encounter us. There, he wishes to reveal himself to us as he did once to Moses, interact with us in loving intimacy as to the most favored of all his children. "*Veni, Domine, visitare nos in pace.*"

The Entrance of Our Lady Into the Temple

*O most Holy One, praised far above the heavens,
you are to become both temple and palace, a true
temple to God to be prepared as the dwelling place
of his coming.*

BYZANTINE LITURGY OF THE FEAST

O n November 21, we celebrate the unique event in the life of a young maiden, Mary, her entrance into the temple, and her total consecration to God. In the Eastern liturgy, Mary, the *Theotokos* ("God-bearer" in Greek), is seen and celebrated as a "living temple of holiness," for it is she who shall one day bear Christ. Again and again she is praised as the "dwelling place of the Almighty," who "contains the Word that cannot be contained." So the young maiden enters into God's temple and is seized by the Holy Spirit, the same Spirit who later shall work the great mystery of the Incarnation in her bosom. Her parents and God's ancestors, Joachim and Anna, carry her into the Holy of Holies, knowing somehow that the maiden's future is already marked by God.

In time and by the action of the Holy Spirit, Mary is to become the living temple of God. The memorial feast we keep today quietly bears witness to that fact. It saddens me somehow that this feast has lessened in character lately in the Western liturgy, for there is so much to learn from the story, and appropriately so, as we ourselves journey on our way to Christmas. Our Lady, as she becomes God's own and unique temple, is a living example for us all. Like her, we, too, are called to become "living temples" of the Holy Spirit, for as Saint Paul reminds us, "whoever is joined to the Lord becomes one spirit with him" (1 Corinthians 6:17).

There is a profound connection between this particular feast and the approaching mystery that shall be revealed at Christmas. Thus, today for the first time we hear during the night

vigil allusions to the Nativity of the Lord. From now until Christmas, the beautiful Christmas canon composed by one of the early Fathers shall be sung on the vigil of major feasts and Sundays. The canon, as it is sung, becomes a living invitation to prepare and be ready for the Lord's arrival. "Christ is born; glorify him! Christ comes from heaven; go out to meet him. Sing to the Lord, all the earth! Praise him with joy, O people, for he has been glorified."

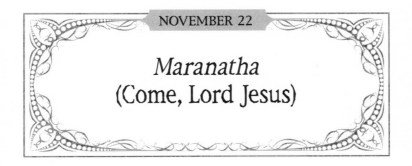

Maranatha
(Come, Lord Jesus)

Come, Lord Jesus, come!

The Advent prayer of the early Church, "Come, Lord Jesus, Come!" is still being answered in new and surprising ways.

STEPHEN BINZ

Advent is a quiet time of waiting and keeping vigil. It is also one of the busiest times of the year, the time for endless hours of shopping and planning the Christmas festivities. There is great contrast between the two, therefore Christians who wish to take Advent and Christmas to heart are called to make serious choices. Instead of wandering around the mall, from shop to shop, the Christian is asked to take time for quiet reflection and reading, and to remain watchful in prayer, eagerly awaiting the coming of the Savior. Humbly but earnestly, filled with faith and confidence, we await the coming of Christ. Deep within us, we hold on to the conviction that his arrival shall bring true peace to the world, the sort of peace that surpasses all human understanding.

As we travel through the sacred season, our desire and prayer for his coming grow in intensity. As the early Christians, we cry out from the depths of our beings, "*Maranatha*, come, Lord Jesus, come!" Right at the beginning of Advent, at its very threshold, the liturgical readings invite us to be on guard and prayerful, keeping continual watch for the Lord's coming.

The whole meaning of Advent seems to be contained in this short prayer: *Maranatha*. It implies that Christ, the Messiah, is the sole object of our desires, the "Desired One" of our hearts,

and so we long for his coming. As we express our longing for him through the frequent *Maranatha* praying, we notice the capacity of our hearts expanding. Saint Bernard explains this phenomenon saying that as our longing and desire for God increases, so does the heart's capacity to receive and welcome him.

As we daily walk our Advent journey, we ought to pause in a timely fashion, breathe deeply the fresh air, and from the bottom of our beings cry out: "*Maranatha*, come, Lord Jesus, come!" The frequent recourse to the prayer would then allow the Lord's presence to take hold of us. Then, in our innermost beings, we shall experience the peace and joy of his intimate visitation.

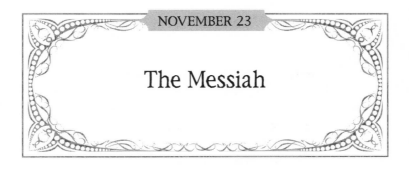

The Messiah

The Messiah, who is called the Christ, is coming,
When he comes, he will teach us everything.
RESPONSORY, FIRST ADVENT WEEK

There I will make a horn sprout for David:
I will set a lamp for my anointed.
His foes I will clothe with shame,
but on him his crown shall shine.
PSALM 132:17–18

he books of the Old Testament, so to speak, are the distillation or narrative of early salvation history, in particular, of the long history of the people of Israel. The Israelites, despite being God's Chosen People, were in many ways just like other folks of the surrounding kingdoms: vulnerable, imperfect, weak, at times even unfaithful to the Lord. And yet, while at times the Lord might have grown impatient and irritated with Israel's infidelities, he never abandoned his people. In fact, he granted them earthly power and a permanent home, the Promised Land, where he established a sure covenant with them. God, always a merciful and kind Father, puts up often with the mistakes and nonsense of his chosen children. He goes as far as announcing through his prophets a plan of salvation and redemption for his people. As the prophets reproach the people of Israel for their infidelities, at the very same time they proclaim to them God's great promise: He will send them a Savior of David's long lineage. It is important to acknowledge that the Savior would be a descendant of David, for, like David, he shall become king and prophet, the very essence of the Messiah. In the Hebrew language, Messiah means "he who has received the unction of God's Spirit," which, translated into Greek, becomes the word *Christos*, that is, Christ.

It was made known to David that his dynasty shall last forever; therefore he prophesies that the Messiah, this descendant of his, would arrive in due time bringing peace and salvation to his people. David calls him "Lord," thus proclaiming the divine origins of the Messiah. From then on, God's covenant with Israel becomes tangible, concrete. It consists on patiently waiting for the "Promised One," the "Anointed One" of God. Henceforth, from generation to generation, a hope in the Messiah becomes the very ethos of the people of Israel. Subsequent prophets continue to announce him, telling the Israelites his time is near—therefore, be prepared! The prophet Micah goes as far as to tell them where the Messiah shall be born: He will be born in Bethlehem as his ancestor David. And Isaiah provides them a sign, totally unintelligible to them: the young woman shall give birth to a son (Isaiah 7:14).

During these blessed Advent days, we, too, are called to imitate the Israelites by cultivating an attitude of strong hope, patiently waiting as they did, for the arrival of the expected Messiah. The reading and prayers in the liturgy, especially the psalms, encourage us to "relive" Israel's eager waiting for the Savior, and to do this in peace and joyful expectation. From the depths of our being we pray for Emmanuel to come be with us and to save us.

From our forefathers the prophets we have learned that the Scriptures are not a series of speculations about metaphysical truths, such as how creation came about or how or when the end of the world shall take place. The Scriptures, as proclaimed, lived, and explained by the prophets, are more an interpretation of divine history, the tale of God inserting himself into it for the sake of saving sinful humanity, the very work of his hands. In the fullness of time, when God sent the "Promised One" into our world, his only Son, the Messiah, there were many who did not recognize him. When Jesus assigned to himself the messianic title by proclaiming the first time he preached in his hometown of Nazareth, "Today this prophecy is here fulfilled..." it instantly became anathema to the many present there in the local synagogue. Time has elapsed since and the centuries have run their course. Through our Christian faith we know that the Messiah, the Christ, has already come once and that he will come again, a second time, at the end of time. It is not a coincidence that today both pious Jews and fervent Christians are still awaiting his coming. Indeed we both have much in common! We are both waiting for the same person! When he comes, his coming shall be a first time for the Jewish people and second time for the Christians. However, for both Jews and Christians, in fact for all people, this shall be his last and final coming. This is our Advent hope and why we find great consolation in our common waiting. "*Veni, Emmanuel!*"

The Advent Icon:
Our Lady of the Sign

*The young woman, pregnant and about to bear a
son, shall name him Emmanuel. Curds and honey
he will eat so that he may learn to reject evil and
choose good.*

ISAIAH 7:14–15

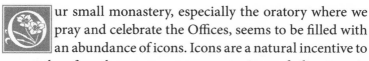ur small monastery, especially the oratory where we
pray and celebrate the Offices, seems to be filled with
an abundance of icons. Icons are a natural incentive to
prayer, therefore, they serve many purposes in our daily monastic
life. The early Church Fathers, such as Saint John Damascene,
saw icons as instrumental in helping the believer enter more
deeply into the mysteries of the faith. The icons accomplish this
by lifting our minds and hearts to the prototype they represent.
In general, most icons depict faithfully the particular biblical
event or mystery they symbolize. In the icon, there is never
room for creative fantasy or a fancy imagination. In its austere
sobriety, the icon and the iconographer never step beyond the
Scriptures or the virtues of the holy person they represent.

Icons are truly vehicles of prayer, for besides instructing us
in the mysteries of the faith, they also embellish God's house

with the beauty of a mysterious supernatural presence. To pray daily in front of an icon is to become aware in a unique way of the presence it represents. During the veneration of icons, a daily experience in our monastic worship, prayerfully we come into physical and spiritual contact with the mystery or person portrayed in the particular icon. This powerful, intangible contact feeds not only our faith, but also our prayer and our piety.

During the Advent season, there is a distinctive icon that holds a central place in our chapel and thus becomes a daily inspiration and object of our veneration. It is the icon of Our Lady of the Sign, as commonly called, based on the words of the prophet Isaiah: "The young woman, pregnant and about to bear a son, shall name him Emmanuel." The inspiration for this icon is the burning bush, which mysteriously prefigures the event of the Incarnation: God enters our humanity and takes possession of it, without absorbing or destroying it. It is in Mary's womb that the Holy Spirit accomplishes the mystery, and this occurs the moment Mary gives her consent to the Angel Gabriel. One of the Byzantine liturgical texts expresses beautifully the mystery represented in this icon:

> *"It is the Lord God, O maiden virgin,*
> *who by the Holy Spirit has conceived in your womb*

and yet you were not consumed.
You, who the burning bush prefigured to Moses, the
     Law-giver.
You were the receptacle of fire,
Of the true fire which can't consume."

Thus, the Our Lady of the Sign icon, as it becomes our cherished companion in our Advent journey, quietly speaks to us of the mysterious union between God and his holy mother, the union that becomes reality in Mary's womb. And this union between the two prefigures another more humble union, for God's Incarnation in Mary makes now possible for us humans to approach and encounter the Lord, not only in the depths of our souls, but in our very flesh when we receive him in holy Communion. Saint Symeon the New Theologian writes splendidly about this mysterious eucharistic union between God and man:

"I share with trembling joy in the divine fire,
I who am only hay,
And oh, such a strange miracle…
Without being consumed I continue to burn
In a beautiful flaming light
As did once, the burning bush."

In the icon of Our Lady of the Sign, Mary, the *Theotokos*, stands beautiful, tall, majestic, noble, with her outstretched arms in a position of constant prayer, pleading, and praise. In the center of her sacred womb stands the Infant Christ surrounded by a large circle, the symbol of his divinity. Mysteriously, he who is the all-infinite and eternal one, by becoming flesh of Mary's womb he enters into our earthly time and space.

Mysteriously but indeed very real, heaven and earth are thus united in the womb of the *Theotokos*, the true God-bearer. The great and unique miracle of the Incarnation, long announced by the prophets: "The young woman, pregnant and about to bear a son..." is today accomplished in the humble womb of a Nazareth maiden.

There are three other icons that are also closely associated with the season of Advent and highly regarded in our monastery: 1) the annunciation icon; 2) the icon of John the Baptist, the forerunner, who points to the Lamb of God; and 3) the icon of the child Emmanuel, enshrined again in a circle and surrounded by angels. The annunciation icon is particularly revealing of God's Incarnation. About nine centuries after David's death, a descendant of his—a humble, quiet virgin from Nazareth— receives a visit from the Archangel Gabriel. She feels confused and beside herself when she hears the Archangel's words uttered to her: "Hail, Mary, full of grace..." He then announces that a son shall be born of her, a son of David; that his conception in her shall be accomplished by the work of the Holy Spirit; and that he shall be the Son of the Most High. Mary, who like all devout Jewish women, knew the Scriptures and recognizes in the Archangel's words the fulfillment of the prophesies concerning the coming of the Messiah. Israel's hope finds its fulfillment in the precious moment Mary pronounces her fiat. In that moment, Mary, in the name of all humanity, welcomes into the human race its author and Creator. In the icon of the annunciation we discover God's promise becomes reality, for at that moment he truly becomes Emmanuel, that is, "God with us!"

"The Word became flesh and made his dwelling among us" (John 1:14).

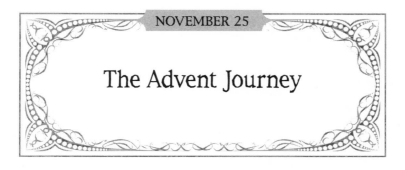

The Advent Journey

I will instruct you and show you the way you should
   walk,
give you counsel with my eye upon you.

PSALM 32:8

Advent is primarily about the coming of God, and
only in a secondary way about our asking, seeking,
waiting, and longing. There is hope, because we are
unconditionally loved, whatever may be our failures,
our tepidity, or our secret despair. The word "Come"
is a bearer of mystery.

MARIA BOULDING, *THE COMING OF GOD*

Some say that ever 'gainst that season comes
Wherein our Savior's birth is celebrated,
The bird of dawning singeth all night long:
And then, they say, no spirit dare stir abroad;
The nights are wholesome, then no planets strike…
So hollow'd and so gracious is the time.

WILLIAM SHAKESPEARE

raveling through the rural country roads of New York's Dutchess County during the early days of winter, some may glimpse from the distance a small, quiet, almost imperceptible monastic building: the monastery of Our Lady of the Resurrection. Perched on a hilltop and surrounded by silent wintry woods, our simple and unpretentious secluded monastic dwelling lies only a few miles away from Millbrook, the nearest village. The brilliant ravishing autumn foliage of autumn has vanished, and the trees stand stark and bare. In early winter I delight in gazing upon the sunset through the elaborate patterns of branches that partition the pink sky like the elegant tracery of a stained-glass window. The trees, with their bare branches reaching quietly toward the sky, toward the dying sunset light, seem to share in the pleading of our Advent prayer: "Come, Lord Jesus, come."

Early Christians traditionally prayed with their arms outstretched toward heaven, from where the Lord was expected to come again. The bare trees with their branches outstretched is a symbolic reminder for the monk and for all Christians, especially during this Advent journey, that we, too, must gaze at all times toward God in unceasing prayer and reach with open arms toward him with deep yearning.

Here in upstate New York, the weather is habitually sharp in early December, sometimes even bitterly cold. Snow may not yet cover the ground, but there is no doubt among us that it is almost winter. Coincidentally, the arrival of the cold in our region corresponds with the arrival of the Advent season in the monastery. For monks, who see themselves on a pilgrimage throughout life, the time of Advent intensifies and deepens the sense of journey. The monastic journey moves forward with expectation toward an arrival, an encounter. The monk, secluded in his monastic desert, longs and prays expectantly for the blessed coming of the Savior, the Lord Jesus Christ.

In the monastery there is something special about Advent, and something of it is felt immediately the moment the vespers hymn "*Conditor Alme Siderum* (Loving Creator of the Stars)" is intoned by the choir. Through the lilting Gregorian melody, one senses the deep feeling of expectation and joy that arrives with the season. From the years of singing repeatedly the same melodies of the monastic chant for either a particular feast or season, they have grown into us, giving the awareness of how beautifully they express the rich meaning of the feast or the season. The endurance of the Gregorian or Byzantine chants, sanctified by centuries of monastic use, have their own unique way of conveying something of the mystery celebrated in

our liturgical prayer. We must never forget the fact that the chant is not music or melody alone, but it is words and music, and the music was written to fit the words, not the other way around, thus making the chant truly a vehicle of prayer. Gregorian Advent melodies, with their simplicity and serene beauty, have a way of transforming our vocal sounds into acts of praise and adoration to God, our Lord and master, for all his wonderful benefits to us.

Among the antiphons of vespers for the first week of Advent, there is one in particular that I find nurtures the Advent message of hope and reflects the loveliness of the season: "*In illa die stillabunt montes dulcedinem* (On that day, the day [of the Lord's coming] sweet wine will flow from the mountains, milk and honey from the hills, alleluia)."

The journey we undertake during Advent is a subtle invitation to climb the Lord's mountain. The journey demands a slow, gradual ascending up the mountain path. As with all uphill climbing, there are certain hazards along the way, but also a joyful expectation of one day reaching the mountaintop, that is, the sacred place where the Lord dwells. The Advent journey reminds us also of another journey: that of our earthly pilgrimage toward communion with God, toward a rich plenitude of life with him. The very character of Advent is to instill in us a vision of our Christian life as a constant pilgrimage, as a dynamic ongoing movement toward a final encounter, and ultimate destination where we enter into the possession of the one our hearts desire.

Advent is certainly a journey, a very real journey that takes us from the forces of darkness and sin into the light of hope and grace. At the beginning, we may undertake the journey with feelings of fear and insecurity. Yet as we continue walking, traveling, and growing into the realization that he who is the object of our destination is also our companion on the road, the landscape of this inner journey begins to change. We discover the joy found in expectancy and patient waiting. We "rejoice with great joy," for we find out, as once did the disciples on the road to Emmaus, that he has been by our side all along. Jesus, as our ultimate judge, is waiting for us at the final moment of the journey, but he, as Savior, is also with us now as we walk through the whole of it.

To truly discern the art of the journey, we must never lose sight of this divine presence who facilitates the journey by driving away those negative elements in our lives: despair, fear, insecurity, sinfulness, superficiality, pride, etc. During the long nights of our Advent journey, we can find comfort in the prayer of the Eastern Church:

"To those who are caught in the night straying into the works of darkness, grant, O Christ, your light and your blessing. Make the path easy for us, whereby we may ascend and so attain to glory" (Byzantine Matins of the Nativity).

NOVEMBER 26

The Advent Wreath

With holly and ivy
So green and so gay,
We deck up our houses
As fresh as the day.

ANONYMOUS, CIRCA 1695

In darkness there is no choice.
It is the light that enables us to see
The differences between things:
And it is Christ who gives us light.

C.T. WHITMELL

very year as we journey into Advent, we notice here in the Northern Hemisphere that our days grow shorter, the air grows colder, and the nights are certainly longer. A quiet stillness sets in on the rural countryside and the nearby Catskill Mountains and hills. And just as Mother Nature retreats into her deepest self during our cold months, the Christian monk is equally invited to turn inward during this blessed Advent period and embark on an inner journey that leads to Christmas. Advent is truly a contemplative season, a time of stillness and quiet, a time when we wait patiently, pray intensely, and prepare eagerly for the arrival of the Light that shall shine on Christmas Day. All of us feel the great need to be rescued from the power of darkness, the somberness and hopelessness that envelop our daily world. There is an instinctual need for light, for the true light that ultimately is revealed on the day of the Lord's coming.

Candles are both symbols and providers of light. Thus in our small monastery they are used in the construction of the Advent wreath. The custom of the Advent wreath—with its

four candles, three purple ones and one pink—originated centuries ago in the northern European countries. The people from the north inherited such customs from the pagan tribes that cultivated the habit of burning lights and building outdoor fires during the time of the winter solstice. It was their way of honoring their gods, of celebrating  the solstice, and also of coping with the darkest month of the calendar: December.

In the sixteenth century, during the time of the Reformation, some Christians conceived the idea of adapting the custom and converting it into a Christian one. The rich symbolism of light adapted itself perfectly to the waiting for the Light during the season of Advent, Christ being the Light of the World. From

Germany, where the custom originated, it spread rapidly to other countries, among both Protestants and Catholics. Eventually, the custom was introduced to monasteries and other regions of the world, and with the first immigrants from those countries it eventually reached America.

Here in the monastery, late in November, we blissfully go out searching throughout the property for the fresh evergreens needed to build the Advent wreath. As we prepare the wreath, we anticipate the joy of lighting the first candle on the evening vigil of the first Sunday of Advent. The lighting of the candle provides us a moment of intense joy and eager anticipation. The peaceful light emanating from the wreath reminds us quietly that the Lord is surely on the way. Every evening, during vespers and also during our evening meal, the ritual of lighting the wreath candles gets repeated. The tiny lights flicking from the candles speak to us of anticipation, of expectation. We are reminded by the candles of Saint Paul's words: "Let us then throw off the works of darkness [and] put on the armor of light" (Romans 13:12). Like the candles pillared and quietly burning in the Advent wreath, our eager hearts are also burning with desire and expectation. Yes, in the words of the Advent liturgy, "We eagerly await the coming of our Savior, the Lord Jesus Christ." Therefore, we try to live in this world with justice, sobriety, and in godly manner, awaiting in hope for the glorious coming of our God. The light from the candles is a reminder to us of this blessed hope we hold onto throughout Advent and thereafter. On Christmas Day, Christ our Light shall appear, and he shall shine like dawn with the splendor and radiance of his beauty.

"Upon you the LORD will dawn, and over you his glory will be seen" (Isaiah 60:2).

NOVEMBER 27

Advent Music

I will praise the LORD all my life,
sing praise to my God while I live.

PSALM 146:2

Let the chant be full of gravity, let it be neither
worldly, not too rude and poor. Let it be sweet, yet
without levity, and, while it pleases the ear, let it
move the heart.

SAINT BERNARD OF CLAIRVAUX

The music of Advent is particularly striking, capable of communicating in a unique way the spirit of the season. One feels sad whenever one must take a trip outside the monastery or go shopping, as happened to me yesterday, and hears endless Christmas tunes blasting all around. I understand people's need for music, particularly during these somber, cold days. It somehow softens the mood and harshness of the weather for them. But I don't think this basic human need is placated by surrounding oneself with Christmas music so early in the season. The tunes create the false impression it is already Christmas when in fact it still is a distance away. This doesn't help us to prepare spiritually for the great feast. Furthermore, when Christmas itself arrives, one feels almost saturated by the sounds of the season.

If we are serious about our own personal Advent journey, we must make the effort to leave cheap entertainment aside and instead search for music in consonance with the spirit of Advent. The season of Advent possesses its own type of inspirational music, music of a rare and haunting beauty. We could listen

to, or better yet sing, the Advent Gregorian melodies: the hymns or antiphons, for instance. Bach's Advent cantatas are worth being listened to repeatedly throughout the season. They stimulate a quiet contemplative mood in synchrony with the season, and they are always an inspiration to prayer. For those who enjoy Handel, there is

the famous *Messiah* oratorio, which conveys splendidly aspects of the mysteries we are reliving through the whole of Advent. I tend to listen to the oratorio toward the end or last Advent days, for I find it in great consonance with the liturgical texts we pray during that time. Then, besides all the serious classical or liturgical music, one also finds a great deal of comfort and inspiration in the popular hymns sung in church or at home, such as: "O Come, O Come, Emmanuel," "People Look East,"

"O Come, Divine Messiah," "Savior of the Nations," and other similar ones. These hymns nurture the Advent spirit of prayerful expectation in both young and old.

Many monasteries have recorded CDs of their Advent music. It is a special joy and inspiration to listen to their chant quietly, prayerfully. As we do so, their prayerful chant becomes part of our own prayer. The Advent texts and music help us to relive and participate interiorly in those crucial moments of salvation history. They also anticipate and expand the inner joy every Christian heart must carry within as it approaches the glorious day of the Nativity, the day when we, too, shall hear the angels announcing the glad tidings to the Bethlehem shepherds and to the people of the surrounding area: "For today in the city of David a savior has been born for you who is Messiah and Lord" (Luke 2:11).

God's Minstrel:
Johann Sebastian Bach

Come, Jesus, come, my flesh is weary,
My strength deserts me more and more.
I yearn for Thy peace;
Life's bitter journey is too hard for me.
Come, I will give myself to Thee,
Thou art the sure Way,
The truth and the Life.

J.S. BACH: MOTET BWV 229

The season of Advent provides us with diverse sources of spiritual food and joy. Among those I find to be of great help, enhancing my inner journey toward Christmas, are the Advent cantatas of Johann Sebastian Bach. One of Bach's greatest gifts, perhaps not always well-known, is that much of his music is principally inspired by faith and thus expresses a profound theology. It is not a surprise, therefore, that some throughout history have called him the Fifth Evangelist.

The inspiration for Bach's music—especially religious music like the cantatas, the Masses, the motets, and the passions—came from his deep, intimate devotion to Christ, his Lord and Savior. This devotion to the Lord was totally consistent with the personal piety encouraged by the Lutheran Church of Bach's time. Although admiring Bach's prodigious creativity and enjoying his music immensely, music lovers often are ignorant of the spiritual inspiration of his music. Bach was a wondrous musician, but he was above all a man of faith, and it was this faith that motivated his great compositions. His music was a vehicle to express the Christian faith that nurtured him and to which he adhered all of his life. Just as religious icons are often referred to as "theology in colors," one could describe Bach's compositions as "theology in music," for it is faith that forms the bedrock of his

music. At the beginning of each of his compositions, Bach usually inscribed the letters SDG: "*Soli Deo Gloria* (to God alone the Glory)." He was always careful to express his personal faith in his music and texts. Bach did not experience a conflict between secular and sacred music, which is often the case with contemporary composers. His faith was totally practical, bringing all aspects of life together and centering them in God, the one source of all good inspiration.

Bach, like many other pious Christians of his time, loved the Bible. Albert Schweitzer, who studied the notations in Bach's personal Bible, described him as "a Christian who lived with the Bible." At reverent performances of music, God is always at hand with his gracious presence.

The Advent cantatas, which I usually listen to in the morning while doing manual work, have become a part of my regular Advent practice throughout the years. These cantatas were primarily written in Leipzig during the many years that Bach was choirmaster of the Church of Saint Thomas, where today he lies buried. As I listen to these cantatas again and again, year after year, they have become a source of spiritual blessing and an inspiration to prayer. Listening to them, one feels immediately drawn to a contemplative, prayerful spirit, a spirit appropriate at all times for a monk, but in particular during the days of Advent. The expectation expressed in the Advent cantatas finds its fulfillment in Bach's *Christmas Oratorio*, which is played often during the Christmas octave here and in many other monasteries around the world.

J.S. Bach has been called "God's greatest musical servant since King David," for what David did with the psalms, Bach accomplished with his music. Bach lived and died faithfully, adhering to the end to the one principle that inspired all of his life: "The aim and fundamental reason of all music is none other than to be the glory of God and the recreation of the human spirit."

> *Jesus, my joy*
> *Delight of my heart,*
> *Jesus, my inspiration;*
> *O how much longer*
> *Must my heart be in anguish*
> *And long for Thee!*
> *Lamb of God, my chosen one,*
> *Nothing on this earth*
> *Can so win my devotion.*

J.S. BACH, MOTET BWV 227

NOVEMBER 29

The Monastery
Advent/Christmas Fair

*Let us remember that the Christmas heart is a giv-
ing heart, a wide-open heart that thinks of others
first. The birth of the Baby Jesus stands as the most
significant event in all history, because it has meant
the pouring into a sick world of the healing medi-
cine of love which has transformed all manners of
hearts for almost two thousand years....Under all
the bulging bundles is this beating Christmas heart.*

GEORGE MATTHEW ADAMS

*From home to home and heart to heart,
from one place to another.
The warmth and joy of Christmas brings us
closer to each other.*

AUTHOR UNKNOWN

There is a long tradition in France that takes place every
year just a few weeks before Christmas called "*le marche
de Noel* (the Christmas market)." It is an old custom not
just in France, but in Germany, Belgium, Spain, Italy, and other
European countries. In the spirit of the season, the people get

seriously engaged in their local annual Christmas fairs. These fairs, depending on the location, are held outdoors whenever possible, just like most farmer's markets, but they also take place indoors, especially in places with inclement weather. They are true community-building events, and the joy of the season, contagious as it usually is, can be felt in the friendly gatherings. The fairs start around mid-November and continue until mid-December or so. All across towns, villages, and monasteries, local people get together to buy gifts, seasonal food, Christmas

decorations, and in particular, the traditional figurines needed for assembling the family crèche. It is a well-known custom that one buys a few figurines at a time, and that most people continue building their crèche collection throughout the years. This is particularly true in Provence, where the native crèche consists not only of the classical Holy Family figures, shepherds and animals, but also includes other personages called "santons": the three Kings, the local baker, the farmer, the seamstress, the priest, the banker, and all other villagers imaginable. Through the use of the Nativity theme and as a way of honoring it, the Provencale people recreate the image and life of their own villages. The "santoniers," as are called the artisans who make the traditional clay figures that are part of the crèche, find a particular joy in recreating and representing their rural people in a variety of forms standing at the scene of Jesus' birth.

Following that old tradition, an annual Christmas craft fair is held here at the monastery every year from the first weekend of Advent to the second. Our annual fair provides to the local people the occasion to admire and sometimes purchase some of the beautiful crèches collected from all over the world. The stables and crèche scenery are built here in the monastery by the monks, by Vassar students doing their internship with us, by former students, and by our volunteers. There are always many crèches to choose from. Some come from distant lands such as Bangladesh, the Philippines, Sri Lanka and, closer to home, Mexico, Honduras, Peru, Ecuador, etc., as well as from France, Germany, Italy, Scandinavia, and China. On occasion we also have available antique crèches that are more than 100 or 150 years old! These crèches, assembled by loving hands throughout the year, become true expressions of the universal character of the mystery of the Incarnation. They witness to the fact that Jesus was born poor, of humble parents, in a simple manger, to save all humankind. They tell the Christmas story, with its universal message of love and its peaceful appeal to all those of good will.

Besides the crèches, other monastic items fabricated here are available to those attending the fair: our vinegars, a product of a long natural fermentation process; products from our gardens such as herbs for cooking and for tea; canned goods such as sauces, soups, chutneys, salsas, tapenade, and jams; and other similar products. We also make available to the public our cookbooks and other spiritual books, as well as Christmas and monastic greeting cards designed here. In the silence and solitude of the monastery, our monastic products are crafted daily with utmost care and attention. All our products use natural materials and are made based on sound artisanal, organic, and ecological principles. Just as other monasteries try to do, we, too, make the effort to create products of quality in the good tradition of Saint Benedict. I am always happy to hear from our friends and clients how much joy they receive from using or offering as gifts our monastic products.

By sharing with others the humble work of our hands, especially during this holy season, we simply seek, in the words of Saint Benedict, "that God may be glorified in all things."

NOVEMBER 30

Feeding the Advent Spirit

Thou hast given so much to me,
Give one thing more—a grateful heart;
Not thankful when it pleaseth me,
As if thy blessings had spare days;
But such a heart, whose pulse may be
Thy praise.

GEORGE HERBERT

The whole thing boils down to giving ourselves in
prayer a chance to realize that we have what we
seek. We don't have to rush after it. It is there all
the time, and if we give it time, it will make itself
known to us.

THOMAS MERTON

We are moving forward with our Advent pilgrimage hoping that not too long from now we shall reach our destination. We tend to seek some comfort and relief from the bleak, frosty days. We must be careful not to try to seek relief from our cold-weather blues by jumping quickly into early Christmas celebrations. Instead of escaping into commonplace, superficial early festivities, we must make every effort to keep the true spirit of Advent in the monastery, in the parish, at home, and, if possible, in the workplace. We can sustain the true spirit of Advent by cultivating practices that enhance the temper of the season. Here are some suggestions:

1. Cultivate an attitude of stillness, of silence, an atmosphere of peace and calm within. This, in turn, fosters inner prayer and recollection.

2. Let us think of our Lady, the expectant mother, and reflect on her attitude of mind and heart while she prepared herself to welcome Jesus on that first Christmas Day. Let our Lady, Saint Joseph, Saint John the Baptist, the prophets, and others be our models during these weeks of Advent. Place an icon of the annunciation in a relevant spot at home to remind yourself of the mystery of the Incarnation, and of the unfailing protection of the *Theotokos*.

3. Make time for reading the Scriptures. God speaks to us through the prophets who announced the coming Messiah. From them, we learn the joyful message of the arrival of the

messianic kingdom. The Scriptures proclaimed in church and during the monastic Offices are rich in symbolism and full of the power of the Holy Spirit. During our long evenings, we can read the book of Isaiah and other parts of the Scripture in the quiet intimacy of our homes. Such a reading feeds our inner journey and is a source of great joy to our souls.

4. Advent has its own music of graceful and profound beauty. We could listen to, or sing, the Gregorian chant melodies of Advent: the hymns, the antiphons, the O Antiphons. Bach's Advent cantatas are an inspiration to prayer, fostering a reflective, contemplative mood very appropriate for the season. There is also Handel's *Messiah*, especially in the last days of Advent. Other popular hymns can also nurture the Advent spirit of joyful expectancy.

5. Participation in the liturgy, in the sacramental life, and the divine mysteries are sources of grace that serve to increase Christ's presence in all of us.

6. Advent, though quiet and introspective, is not a season of gloom and sadness. Rather, it is full of expectant joy. We may delay putting up the Christmas tree and decorations, but we can replace them with a beautiful and simple Advent wreath with its four candles, each lighted progressively during the four weeks of the celebration. We can pray, read, sing, and eat by the Advent wreath. Lighting one of its candles is a moment filled with promise, peace, and longing, for we know that the hour of our liberation is at hand. In the words of the liturgy, we pray: "Come, and deliver us, O Lord. Come, do not delay."

7. In our refectory, a small crèche is placed in a prominent place at the start of Advent, but without the statue of the Infant Jesus. A candle next to it is lit during the evening meal. The empty crib in the crèche is a constant reminder, in the words of the Christmas antiphon, that "the Eternal Word emptied himself for our sake and became man." It also increases our yearning to see his face on Christmas Eve when just before the singing of the Solemnity's first vespers the Infant Jesus is placed in the crèche and the Christmas tree is lit.

8. We must be particularly faithful to praying the daily Angelus—the great prayer of the mystery of the Incarnation.

9. Let us remember the needs of the poor, the lonely, the aged, and those most abandoned. They are God's favorite people, and the Lord often visits us through them. He said: "Whatsoever you have done to the least of my brethren, you have done it unto me." Ironically, the same season that brings celebrations of plenty to many can also mean a time of meager resources for those who find themselves in a bind, often having the difficult choice to make between a warm house or a warm meal.

10. Let us cultivate a grateful heart toward God and toward others. Let's express our gratitude to the Lord for the common, ordinary gifts of everyday life, as well as for the spiritual gifts this holy season brings upon us. Lets us be thankful to God for family and friends, for health and well-being, for peace in the world and our surroundings, and especially for the care, kindness, and concern of others. Let us, in Saint Paul's words, remain thankful in all things. *Deo gratias!*

The Wonder of the Incarnation

From a sermon by Saint Gregory Nazianzus (paraphrased)

he very Son of God, who existed before the ages, he is the invisible one, the incomprehensible, the incorporeal, the beginning of beginning, the light of light, the fountain of life and immortality, the image of the archetype, the immovable seal, the perfect resemblance, the definition and living word of the Father; he it is who comes to his own image and embraces our nature for the good of our own nature and unites himself to an intelligent soul for the good of my soul, to purify like by like. The Son of God absorbs in himself all that is human, except sin. He is conceived in the womb of the Virgin Mary, who had been first prepared in soul and body by the Holy Spirit; his birth is treated with honor, and virginity is received with new honor. He comes forth as God, in the human nature he has absorbed, one being, made of two opposite elements, flesh and spirit, spirit gives diversity, flesh receives it.

"He who is wealth itself is made poor; he takes on the poverty of our flesh that we may gain the wealth of his divinity. He who is fullness in himself accepts to become empty; he empties himself for a brief period of time, that we all may share in his fullness. We need God to take our flesh and die that we might love. We died with him that we may be purified. We rise again with him, because we have died with him. We are glorified with him, because we have risen again with him."

During these incipient Advent days we nourish our faith and stimulate our hearts and minds by remaining faithful to our daily sacred reading, in particular the prophets and the Fathers. They are our daily companions on our Advent journey. They feed and sustain us as pilgrims on the road. It is sad, indeed, to acknowledge that many Christians never read the books of the Old Testament or some of the early Church Fathers. They forget, somehow, that Christ is truly present in the events and writings of the Old Testament, especially in the prophets' writings. When we hear the prophetic word, it is the Lord himself who is speaking to our hearts. Christ once reproached the disciples on the way to Emmaus for being "fools and slow of heart in believing and accepting all that the prophets have spoken." Both the prophets and the Fathers are God's messengers, and with their solid teachings they somehow help us in deciphering the inner contents of God's message.

The Holy Spirit

Come, let us rejoice in the Holy Spirit!
Let us sing endless praises to Christ our God!
Let us celebrate the joy of Joachim and Anna,
The conception of the Mother of God,
For she is the fruit of the grace of God.

VESPERS HYMN FOR THE CONCEPTION OF THE *THEOTOKOS*

uring these peaceful and calm Advent days, there is a mysterious presence felt in our prayers and readings, a presence of whom little is spoken. It is the subtle, mysterious, almost incomprehensible presence of the Holy Spirit. We know through faith that from all eternity, in the intimate council of the Holy Trinity, the Holy Spirit was assigned the work of the Incarnation. It was by his mighty power that the Son of God became incarnate in the Virgin Mary. The Incarnation of God's Son, willed by the Father long before the ages began and totally assented by the Son himself, is the particular and unique operation of the Holy Spirit.

The more we immerse ourselves in the work of prayer, the more we come to discover something about the Holy Spirit's presence in our lives. "It is one thing to believe in God," Staretz

Silouan used to say, "and another to know him." It is in prayer, and by the direct action of the Holy Spirit, that we come to understand something of the mystery of the Incarnation, of the two natures of Christ: divine and human. Only the Holy Spirit can communicate to the praying believer something of that splendid divine union of two different natures and two wills. Infused divine knowledge is a gift from the Holy Spirit, and it is his divine power that opens our hearts and minds to this type of knowledge.

It is through experiencing the Holy Spirit interiorly, deep, deep within our souls, that the mystery of Jesus Christ is revealed to us. The Holy Spirit confers on us both faith and grace to arrive at this divine knowledge. Advent is a special time to keep close to the Holy Spirit (though we know through faith, all times are his and belong to him!). But Advent and Christmas are periods of abundant graces that flow from the inner life of the blessed Trinity. These graces are channeled into our hearts through the power and grace of the Holy Spirit. Humbly, patiently, the Holy Spirit pursues each of us, gradually revealing his divine presence to us, eagerly preparing our hearts to become a worthy manger for the Savior.

Any relationship with God is impossible apart from the Holy Spirit. It is the Holy Spirit who points us to the revelation of Christ. It is the light from the Holy Spirit that illumines our understanding and allows us to apprehend something of that love that instigated the Father to send his beloved and only begotten Son into the world. For indeed, God so loved the world that in the fullness of time, by the action of the Holy Spirit, he sent his Anointed One to be born of a humble maiden in the small forsaken village of Bethlehem. As Christians, as humble disciples of Jesus, we live and have communion with God by unction from the Holy Spirit. The Holy Spirit breathes Christ, the full Christ, into our lives. By this very fact he establishes us in that mysterious communion of love with the Father, and the Son, and the Holy Spirit. "*Veni, Sancte Spiritus.*"

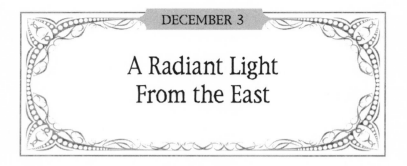

A Radiant Light From the East

People look East, the time is near
Of the crowning of the year.
Make your house fair as you are able,
Trim the hearth and set the table.
People look East, and sing today:
Love, the Lord, is on the way.

EIGHTEENTH-CENTURY CAROL
FROM BESANCON, FRANCE

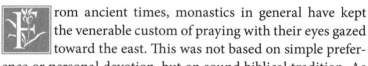

rom ancient times, monastics in general have kept the venerable custom of praying with their eyes gazed toward the east. This was not based on simple preference or personal devotion, but on sound biblical tradition. As we read in the Gospel of Matthew: "For just as the lightning comes from the east and is seen as far as the west, so will the coming of the Son of Man be" (Matthew 24:27).

Our monastic oratory is built facing the east, and during these early days of Advent, I am struck at how appropriate it is that we continue to preserve this ancient, venerable, and wise custom of praying toward the east. A life-size icon of the Christ Pantokrator, enrobed in majesty, presides in the apse of our chapel, surrounded on each side by the icons of the Mother of God and John the Baptist. Both of them, with their hands pointing to the Lord, make quiet intercession for all of us. In Greek the triptych icons together are called "The *Deesis,*" that is, "The Intercession." The Lord, clothed in glory and majesty, looks with gravity at us, while Mary, the *Theotokos,* and John, God's herald, silently plead our cause.

During our Advent journey, I hold on to the vision expressed in the *Deesis* icon. The mystery of Advent tells me that Christ became incarnate in time, became part of our human race and history, and revealed to us what lies beyond time, awaiting all of us. The vision holds a promise that, at the end of time, when the Lord of glory appears from the east, as Savior and judge, we, his disciples, shall hear the glad tidings from his mouth: "Come, you who are blessed by my Father. Inherit the kingdom prepared for you from the foundation of the world" (Matthew 25:34). These words from the Gospel are particularly consoling to hear during our Advent days, filled as they are with earthly cares and busy Christmas preparations. They bespeak of the *beata pacis visio,* the "blissful vision of peace" promised to all of us in the new Jerusalem, where the kingdom of God will be fully realized. "Our Savior, the Dayspring from the East, has visited us from on high, and we who were in darkness and shadow have found the truth: for the Lord is born of the Virgin" (Exapostilarion Matins of the Nativity of the Lord).

The Magnificat

And Mary said:
"My soul proclaims the greatness of the Lord;
my spirit rejoices in God my savior."

LUKE 1:46–47

aily at vespers, before concluding our evening Office, we stand up and solemnly sing the Magnificat, Mary's song of praise. I am always strongly drawn to this particular moment in the Office and to every word uttered in the Magnificat. It is interesting to note that the evangelist Luke places the Magnificat in his Gospel in the context of Mary's visitation (which Luke describes immediately following the annunciation) to her cousin Elizabeth, whom she went to help for a period of three months. Elizabeth had conceived a child in her old age, and was much in need of assistance, so Mary departed in haste from Nazareth to render service to her cousin.

Every year, and appropriately so, we read during Advent the Gospel account of the visitation. In that reading, we learn to distill the meaning of every word sung in proclamation by our Lady in her Magnificat. For Mary has just concluded a most unusual and astonishing encounter with the Angel Gabriel. Now, she hastily travels to a small Judean town to aid Elizabeth. She was bursting with emotion, almost confused at the mystery that was just accomplished in her. When she arrives at Zechariah's house and encounters her cousin, the child in Elizabeth's womb leaped for joy. Filled with the Holy Spirit, Elizabeth bursts into a loud exclamation saying, "Most blessed are you among women, and blessed is the fruit of your womb. And why does this happen to me, that the mother of my Lord should come to me?... Blessed are you who believed that what was spoken to you by the Lord would be fulfilled" (Luke 1:42–43, 45). Upon hearing

Elizabeth's greetings, Mary, otherwise always calm and composed, can no longer contain her deep feelings and she in turn bursts into a song of praise acknowledging the mighty deeds the Lord had just accomplished in her. Her soul, filled with gratitude for the Almighty, breaks into this song of praise:

"My soul proclaims the greatness of the Lord;
my spirit rejoices in God my savior."

And in her song, Mary recalls her own personal history, her own dealings with the Almighty from whom she had received everything:

"For he has looked upon his handmaid's lowliness;
behold, from now on will all ages call me blessed."

And with that extreme humility of hers, the very humility that caught God's eyes and attracted his attention, she acknowledges once more God's lavish favors bestowed upon her:

> *"The Mighty One has done great things for me,*
> *and holy is his name."*

Our Lady confirms a truth she had learned from the prophets of old, and from the psalmist in particular, that "merciful and gracious is the LORD, slow to anger, abounding in mercy" to all those who fear him. God's merciful love, which so magnificently was manifested to Mary, she makes clearly known that this extends to all those who fear the Lord. For as the prophet taught, "the fear of the LORD is the beginning of wisdom." Thus Mary celebrates God's mercy for the people of Israel, for those who delight in the Lord and keep his commands:

> *"His mercy is from age to age*
> *to those who fear him.*
> *He has shown might with his arm,*
> *dispersed the arrogant of mind and heart."*

Not surprisingly, Mary, who acknowledges God's preference for the humble, clearly states the truth contained on the other side of the coin: God's distaste for the proud and the conceited, the Lord's total displeasure with self-centered people who delight in their own selves and who, in their pride, attribute all good to themselves. Mary points out the contrast in how the Lord deals with the proud-hearted and how he acts toward the humble:

> *"He has thrown down the rulers from their thrones*
> *but lifted up the lowly."*

Mary states clearly without any doubt something we should hear later, again and again, from the lips of her Son: "The hungry he has filled with good things; the rich he has sent away empty," that is, God's preferential treatment for the poor. No need here to get into contemporary theological disputes or controversies; Christ's own words should suffice. His own authority, applying Isaiah's words to himself that "he has sent me to bring good news to the afflicted." The experience of poverty, from birth to death, marked Jesus' life and thus also that of his mother. In the Magnificat, Mary simply recalls for our benefit God's special welcome of the poor and lowly:

"The hungry he has filled with good things;
the rich he has sent away empty."

Mary returns to the theme of mercy, reminding us again that God alone is the all-merciful one, and one day her Son, Christ the merciful, shall also be our judge. Just as much as he forgave Israel's infidelities because of his great mercy, we can also count on his loving mercy for our own personal lives. When we pray with Mary, the *Theotokos*, we are to remember her Son's daily gift of his great mercy:

> *"He has helped Israel his servant,*
> *remembering his mercy."*

And finally, our Lady and Mother reminds us that at all times God keeps the covenant made with his people. In the last days, in the fullness of time, he sent us a Savior, a Redeemer, the complete fulfillment of his promise. With Mary and Joseph, with Elizabeth and Zechariah, with Abraham, David and our older ancestors, the prophets and the patriarchs, with the whole people of Israel, we rejoice and are thrilled with gladness that God's promise is being realized in our midst:

> *"According to his promise to our fathers,*
> *to Abraham and to his descendants forever."*

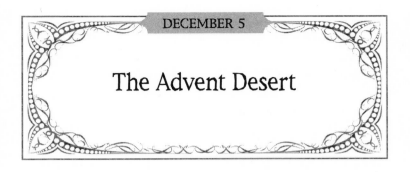

The Advent Desert

"What did you go out into the desert to see?..."
"Why did you go out?"

MATTHEW 11:7, 9

It was in the desert that Israel had come to know
God.

CARL KAZMIERSKI: *JOHN THE BAPTIST: PROPHET AND EVANGELIST*

The desert is not a place of isolation, but one of
encounter.

ANDRÉ NEHER, 1988

dvent, in a subtle way, plunges us directly and without hesitation into the desert experience. The desert is not a sentimental or romantic place to dream about; it is bare, austere, empty, desolate, and there is no place to hide in its confines. It is just what it is: the desert. Advent, similar to Lent in many ways, implies and really requires a sojourn into the depths of the desert. Like John the Baptist, God asks us to journey into the desert for a very specific purpose: to prepare the way for the Lord. More than ever, we need to find ourselves in an empty place, in the bare reality of the wilderness. We are too busy otherwise—like Martha, "worried about many things"—to adequately provide our undivided attention to "only one thing." The desert helps us to strip off all unwarranted necessities and face squarely our own sinful reality, our naked and broken humanity, in utter need of redemption.

John the Baptist grew up in the wilderness. This rather stark desert figure seemed to have intimidated many. His austere message of repentance was a two-edged sword to those who listened

to him. And yet, precisely because of it, he was chosen by the Almighty to prepare the way for the Lord. He thus became "the voice of one crying out in the desert," the one called to make straight the path leading to God's "Anointed One."

"Behold, I am sending my messenger ahead of you; he will prepare your way." From John the Baptist we learn the desert is a place for cleansing, for conversion, for fasting, for silence, for self-discovery, and ultimately for healing. It is a place to let go of our multiple earthly attachments, making room for the Lord by allowing God to enter fully into the innermost of our lives, yes, of our broken lives in utter need of his compassion and healing.

The desert is also the place for pursuing the "patient waiting" attitude that God demands from each of us. This patient waiting attitude is similar in many ways to that "patient endurance" counseled by the Apostle Paul. It demands true patience, and it also means hard work. This patient waiting attitude is inspired by deep faith and trust in God, and is the work of constant prayer under the guidance of the Holy Spirit. During this time of patiently waiting for the Lord's arrival, he asks from each of us complete trust and openness to his particular designs for our lives, complete and total cooperation with that which he wishes to accomplish in us. When Christmas, the Lord's day, arrives, we shall then discover the truth of the prophetic words: "The wilderness and the parched land (of our hearts) will exult; the Arabah (desert) will rejoice and bloom" (Isaiah 35:1).

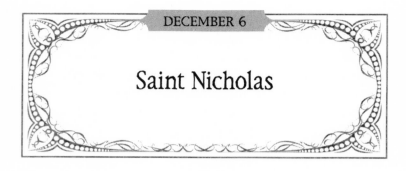

DECEMBER 6

Saint Nicholas

All of you who love to celebrate,
Come and sing the praises of the most noble of
    bishops,
The glory of the ancient fathers,
A fountain of wonders and great protector of the
    poor.
Rejoice, faithful helper of the afflicted,
And fervent advocate of those who are oppressed.
O, holy bishop Nicholas,
Never cease to intercede with Christ our God,
For those who honor your blessed memory
With faith and love.

BYZANTINE VESPERS VERSES FOR THE FEAST OF SAINT NICHOLAS

Saint Nicholas, the most human of saints, was always ready to help where need existed. By his very humanity, the saint reflected popular hopes and fears. He changed because human needs changed.

MARTIN EBON, *SAINT NICHOLAS: LIFE AND LEGEND*

arly in Advent, a season that speaks to us of hope and of the great efforts we must make to lead honest Christian lives, we celebrate the feast of Saint Nicholas (December 6). His feast is an important pause on our Advent journey, a time to reflect and ponder on Saint Nicholas' admirable example of Gospel living. There is much in his life that Christians of all times and places, be they from the East or the West, North or South, can learn from him.

Among the several icons of saints that adorn our humble monastic chapel with their holy presence, the icon of Saint Nicholas stands out brightly. Because my place in the chapel is almost right in front of the icon, I have occasion several times a day to gaze on it while I am at prayer. What is particularly striking about this icon is the fact that the saint is not represented alone. Saint Nicholas is in the center with arms outstretched in a gesture of prayer, and all around him, as almost framing his presence, are episodes of the many good deeds he performed and the many people he helped during his lifetime.

I can't help but think how appropriate it is for Christians today to reflect on the humble example of Saint Nicholas. His life, a rather ordinary one, was given entirely to prayer and good works. He was not a monk, writer, or teacher, but he preached daily to his people the word of God and lived by it. He battled for the rights of the poor and oppressed and vigorously defended the rights of widows and orphans. One could easily describe Saint Nicholas today as a saint with a certain social conscience.

Like Christ, his Lord and master, Saint Nicholas was a good shepherd to his flock, exercising special compassion and mercy toward the outcasts, the poor, the undesirables of his time, and all those who were in distress in one form or another. His gentle goodness and exemplary life radiated beyond the frontiers or limits of his own diocese of Myra, attracting pagans and unbelievers to the revelation of Jesus Christ, the Messiah.

The life of Saint Nicholas is an exemplary Gospel witness for our times, not just as we get ready ourselves for Christmas, but as our entire lives unfold under a societal climate not unlike that of the time of Saint Nicholas. His example and preaching, totally in accord with the Lord's teachings in the Gospels, is the antithesis of the rhetoric of meanness and self-centeredness preached by many politicians today: that the poor, the elderly, the undocumented immigrants, the marginal, etc., are enemies for whom compassion is too costly. In such times, intolerance of those who appear different from the social norm because of race, age, language, nationality, or sexual orientation is countenanced. It saddens me deeply that some who espouse such policies call themselves Christians, when these ideas are in direct opposition to the teachings of Jesus, the master. All we have to do is read Matthew 25:31–46 to be reminded where the Gospel stands on these matters. And what an irony, that these same people would make claims to being exemplary Christians, people of faith and prayer, people who spend their days honoring God, yet in practice would not honor the very words and example from the master: "Whatever you did for one of these least brothers of mine, you did for me." They should be reminded of the Lord's harsh words to people who act in similar fashion: "Hypocrites, well did Isaiah prophesy about you when he said:

> *'This people honors me with their lips,*
> *but their hearts are far from me;*
> *in vain do they worship me,*
> *teaching as doctrines human precepts'"*

MATTHEW 15:7–9

Political ideologies or labels don't mean very much in monastic life. Christian monks in general leave behind worldly concerns in order to follow Jesus. But though politics may mean little to us, policies mean a great deal, as they should to all Christians. Policies usually either promote or are in opposition to the values of the Gospel. It is our duty, therefore, not only to pray, but even to speak out on occasion, when needed, for the sake of the Gospel. In a chaotic and selfish world, where greed, hatred, intolerance, punishment, revenge, and discrimination become the exalted values of a society, the Christian, like Saint Nicholas, must gently but firmly proclaim the love and selflessness of Jesus, the peace, compassion, and mercy of the Gospel. We must look at the present political and cultural climate in our country and the entire world, as Saint Nicholas, the humble disciple of the Lord would: as a challenge from God to take the Gospel seriously and to proclaim it with our very lives. This is the grace we must pray and ask Saint Nicholas on his feast day.

Holy Father Nicholas,
Healer of the sick,
Liberator of captives,
Treasure of the poor,
Consoler of the afflicted,
And guide to travelers.
Be always a living symbol
of the Savior's love and
mercy for all of us.

DECEMBER 7

Advent Longing

Be thou my vision, O Lord of my heart,
Naught be all else to me save that thou art;
Be thou my best thought in the day and night,
Waking or sleeping thy presence my light.
EIGHTH-CENTURY IRISH CELTIC POEM

The shorter days of late autumn make the Advent reality a stark and reflective one. It turns us inward, as it intensifies our hope, our longing, and our patient waiting for the Messiah. Through active faith and much prayer, we struggle to purify and cleanse our desires, for we wish to be properly prepared and in good form for the arrival of the Lord at Christmas. We simply can't take for granted this most unusual gift of God's imminent coming to us. An arrival/coming never dreamed of in olden times, an arrival that shall change the course of history forever. Through the mystery of this divine/human birth in our midst, God's own personal visitation to our world, the face of humanity is transfigured, redeemed, and changed forever. Nothing will ever be the same!

Advent is an evocative time to reflect and cultivate a deep yearning, a most passionate longing for the Lord, for he who is to come doesn't come in vain: He wishes foremost to be born in the innermost of our hearts. Saint Anselm, in his *Proslogion* (discourse on the existence of God), expresses beautifully the sentiments that we should make our own at this time:

"Enter into your mind's inner chamber. Shut out everything but God and whatever helps you to seek him; and when you

have shut the door, look for him. Speak now to God and say with your whole heart: I seek your face. Lord, I desire you. Teach me to seek you, and when I seek you show yourself to me, for I cannot seek you unless you teach me, nor can I find you unless you show yourself to me. Let me seek you in desiring you and desire you in seeking you, find you in loving you, and love you in finding you."

This longing, this profound yearning for the Lord's coming, purifies our hearts and enhances our daily prayer in a very special way. It also bestows in us the Holy Spirit's power to drive away all those negative thoughts, feelings, images, and ugly passions that are totally incompatible with a worthy preparation for Christ's arrival. "*Ecce, ego venio et habitabo in medio tui.*"

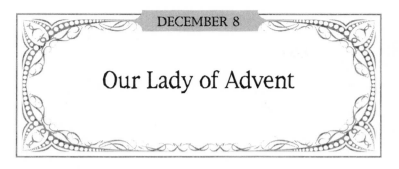

Our Lady of Advent

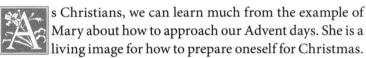

When his mother Mary was betrothed to Joseph,
but before they lived together, she was found with
child through the holy Spirit.

MATTHEW 1:18

As Christians, we can learn much from the example of Mary about how to approach our Advent days. She is a living image for how to prepare oneself for Christmas. The presence of the Mother of God can be felt quietly in our hearts as we make our tiny efforts to walk the Advent journey in her company. Our Lady is the perfect companion in the journey toward meeting Christ, her beloved Son, for she is the humble servant who now carries him within. From the moment she receives the good news from the Archangel Gabriel about the mission God intended for her, she accepts her role with utter humility and simplicity. She does not attribute anything to herself. She simply obeys God's plan for her and submits entirely to the work of God's Holy Spirit. When Gabriel arrives at her modest home in Nazareth, he finds a humble maiden waiting, ready to accept whatever the Lord's design holds for her.

After the Archangel delivers his message, she tells him:

"Behold, I am the handmaid of the Lord. May it be done to me according to your word" (Luke 1:38). She demands nothing from God's messenger. On the contrary, she accepts everything expected of her and in return she receives everything by the power of the Holy Spirit. The great mystery is accomplished in her, and the Word becomes flesh in her by taking her own flesh. Thus, the Son of God the Most High becomes also the Son of Mary, the humble maid. She who was poor, quiet, and totally empty of herself now possesses all: God himself. From now on, thousands of generations shall call her blessed.

Our Lady of Advent is without any doubt a unique model of how to embrace and love the true Advent spirit as we continue on our road to Christmas. She lived her own Advent for nine months, a longer period than our short four to eight weeks. She also lived it in greater intimacy, for he whom we expect to come dwelled within her, and she nourished and cared for him with unsurpassed love. The lowly, prayerful, humble, quiet waiting attitude exercised by our Lady during her own Advent exemplifies what all our Advent days should be like. In the midst of the noisy and often chaotic Christmas preparations we encounter in today's world, the example of the Mother of God stands apart from all that is false, haughty, glittering, selfish, or superficial. Mary's presence in our midst, radiating a serene beauty through her silence, her acceptance, and total submission to God's plan, speaks volumes to each and every one of us. What profound lessons we can all learn from her. Like the *Theotokos*, each of us is also called to accept God's personal plans for our lives and to surrender to him. Like Mary, we, too, are called to better our lives not once, but many times as the Lord reveals his will in our daily lives. Like our Lady, we must live our own submissions to the Lord with complete simplicity, humility, and trust in his plan for each of us.

> *Of her flesh he took flesh:*
> *He does take, fresh and fresh,*
> *Though much the mystery how.*
> *Not flesh but spirit now,*
> *And wakes, O marvelous!*
> *New Nazareth in us,*
> *Where we shall yet conceive*
> *him, morning, noon, and eve;*
> *New Bethlehem, and he born*
> *There, evening, noon, and morn.*

GERALD M. HOPKINS

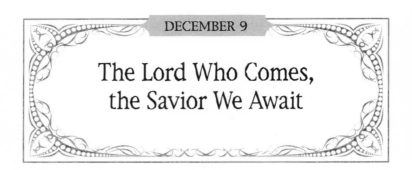

The Lord Who Comes, the Savior We Await

See how glorious he is, coming forth,
*   as Savior of all peoples.*

VESPERS ANTIPHON, FOURTH SUNDAY OF ADVENT

Behold, the time of our salvation is near,
Prepare yourself, O cavern,
For a Virgin Mother approaches to give birth to a
*   Son.*
Rejoice and be glad, O Bethlehem, land of Judea,
For in you the Lord shall shine forth as the dawn.
Give ear, you mountains and hills
And all lands surrounding Judea.
For Christ is coming to save the people
He has created and whom he loves.

SUNDAY BYZANTINE VESPERS BEFORE THE NATIVITY

dvent is all about the coming of God in our midst. This sense of Christ's approaching as the Savior of all is what gives Advent its distinct and special character. Of course we know indeed that Christ already came some 2,000 years ago, but what Advent does is to renew the awareness of his presence among us. The grace of Advent also intensifies our longing for the Lord, for our full communion with him.

Advent helps us relive anew, each year, the mystery of the Incarnation, of Christ coming in the flesh on that first Christmas. Just as he came long ago into the womb of Mary, his mother, and later, on Christmas Day, to the world at large, so now he comes again to be reborn in our hearts. Through the grace of the sacraments, especially the Eucharist, he penetrates our innermost selves. Advent also brings to mind that other coming of the Lord, his final coming in glory, reminding us that we must become like the vigilant servant of the Gospel, always ready for Christ's return. We anticipate this Second Coming in joy, praying as the first Christians did: Come, Lord Jesus, come.

The Gospel according to Matthew assigns several titles to the Lord whom we eagerly await: Messiah, Savior, Son of God, Emmanuel. These titles, in the eyes of the evangelist, clearly delineate the specific roles he is to fulfill. By his human conception of David's lineage and divine conception by the Holy Spirit, Jesus is recognized, proclaimed, as the Messiah and Son of God the Most High. By calling him Savior, Saint Matthew is reminding us that this tiny child one day will deliver his people from their sins. And by bestowing on him the name Emmanuel, "God with us," he assures us once more that God, according to his promise, will remain always with his people. *Iuste et pie vivamus, expectantes beatam spem et adventum Domini.*

DECEMBER 10

Advent Vigilance

Christ our judge commands us to be vigilant. We wait expectantly for his holy visitation for he comes to be born of a virgin.

COMPLINE, PREFEAST OF THE NATIVITY

It is the hour now for you to awake from sleep. For our salvation is nearer now than when we first believed; the night is advanced, the day is at hand.

ROMANS 13:11–12

The practice of inner vigilance puts us in a perfect Advent mood. There is nothing closer to the true Advent spirit than a vigilant attitude. Indeed, vigilance is a very Christian, very monastic virtue. The monastic day starts with the praying of vigils. Early in Advent, one of the Church readings reminds us of Jesus' words: "Do not let the Lord come suddenly and catch you asleep…be therefore vigilant, on the guard." This admonition from the Scriptures is a strong reminder of the need for constant vigilance. To cultivate an inner, vigilant attitude means to remain continually on the alert for all those signs the Lord provides us daily. They encourage us to persevere in our Advent resolutions and seek his presence in all of life's circumstances.

Be alert, be vigilant, be on the guard: This means keeping our hearts in a state of constant readiness. We know, as he himself reminds us, sometimes the Lord comes "like a thief at night." Advent vigilance challenges us to be ready at all times for his coming. Vigilance urges us to be prepared, for the Lord is close at hand.

Vigilance is central to a humble, prayerful, and meaningful Advent observance. We keep vigil and patiently wait, as we beseech the Lord to come and fully enter into our lives. It is true that Christ comes to us not only at Christmas, but even at all times, daily; nevertheless his coming at Christmas is a very special one. It is one filled with the intensity of our desires, the longing for our redemption, a vivid and most inspiring coming full of the grace and joy. Our Advent vigilance reminds us often that Jesus, the Messiah and our Savior, is indeed very near us and that, likewise, we are also very near and dear to him. "*Veni Domine, et noli tardare.*"

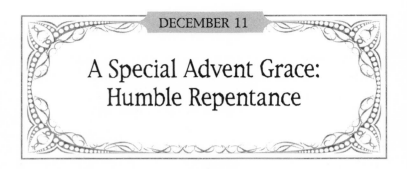

DECEMBER 11

A Special Advent Grace:
Humble Repentance

Long is our winter, dark is our night;
Come, set us free, O saving Light.
Come, set us free, O saving Light,
Come, dwell among us, O Son of God.

XV HYMN

During the second and third weeks of Advent, we are plunged deep in the middle of our "Advent-desert experience." Through the words of the precursor we hear an invitation to what is to be our Advent undertaking for the remaining days of the journey: "Repent, / prepare the way of the Lord, / make straight his paths." The call to humble repentance, to conversion, is our task at hand.

Advent is a special time for improving mutual relationships, in this case, the reciprocal friendship that exists between God and us. It is a time of grace, given by God to strengthen that unique connection that binds us to him. God freely pours his grace into our hearts through his Holy Spirit, and in return he expects our total cooperation, our humble submission through grateful repentance. John the Baptist's message to us is clear: We must walk the ways of repentance, of personal conversion, and thus prepare the way for the Lord. We can only prepare a worthy place for God inside ourselves by sincerely embracing the humble and lowly state of repentance. In the Baptizer's words and in those of the prophet Isaiah: "Every valley shall be filled and every mountain and hill shall be made low"; that is, we are called to remove all obstacles and impediments to smooth out his path by tearful repentance. Only then can the Lord take possession of us in complete freedom.

In the days of John the Baptist, his austere message resounded straightforward with utmost decisiveness in the sterile desert. As such, it is also important for us to journey into our own desert and heed his message in the innermost part of our hearts. It is there that God is patiently waiting for us, that he wishes to come closer to us by our turning to him through the process of an honest conversion and sincere repentance. Furthermore, it is there that he wishes to communicate with us, in the silent and humble seclusion of our repenting hearts. Once we reach that very special and lowly place, he shall reveal himself and interact with us lovingly, thus deepening the divine relationship that is the cause of our joy.

Have mercy on me, God, in accord with your merciful love;
in your abundant compassion blot out my transgressions.
Thoroughly wash away my guilt;
and from my sin cleanse me.
Against you, you alone have I sinned;
I have done what is evil in your eyes...

PSALM 51

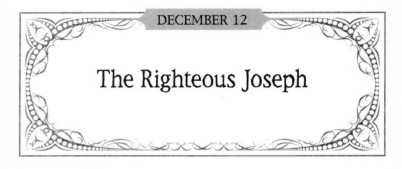

The Righteous Joseph

Now this is how the birth of Jesus Christ came about. When his mother Mary was betrothed to Joseph, but before they lived together, she was found with child through the holy Spirit. Joseph her husband, since he was a righteous man, yet unwilling to expose her to shame, decided to divorce her quietly. Such was his intention when, behold, the angel of the Lord appeared to him in a dream and said, "Joseph, son of David, do not be afraid to take Mary your wife into your home. For it is through the holy Spirit that this child has been conceived in her. She will bear a son and you are to name him Jesus, because he will save his people from their sins."

MATTHEW 1:18–21

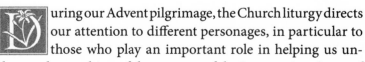uring our Advent pilgrimage, the Church liturgy directs our attention to different personages, in particular to those who play an important role in helping us understand something of the mystery of the Incarnation. Some of these imminent figures are our Lady, Gabriel the archangel, the ancient prophets (in particular Isaiah, David, and also Micah),

John the Baptist and his parents, Elizabeth and Zechariah, and last but not least, Saint Joseph, the righteous man. Of all those personages here mentioned, it is Joseph, the righteous carpenter from Nazareth, who seemed to have played the greatest role, after our Lady, in the birth and rearing of the Child Jesus. It is Joseph, the righteous, who is commanded by the angel to protect and safeguard the life of the tiny child and his mother.

Saint Joseph the righteous man comes across in the Gospel as quiet, hidden, almost inconsequential, doing simply the job assigned to him and this in an almost imperceptible manner. His role during the birth of Christ is ignored by many because of the unostentatious fashion in which he went about his business—not a single one of his utterances is recorded in the Gospel account of the Nativity. He was basically a man of faith, a man of total obedience to God's commands; thus he didn't need to make noise or fuss about himself to carry out what was asked of him. By not fussing about himself, Joseph could give his undivided attention and care to the two most important people in his life, Jesus and Mary. Joseph is, above all, the humble servant of the Lord. During our Advent days, he is in many ways a sure guide on our journey to Christmas. He is a model of what we also are called to be: obedient servants of the Lord. Saint Joseph and Mary, his bride, in giving their total humble obedience to the Lord, paradoxically received at the same time the homage and complete obedience of the Son of God to them.

> *Righteous Joseph, Son of David,*
> *Foster father and protector of Jesus,*
> *Spouse of Mary, ever Virgin,*
> *Watch over and guide the vineyard of the Lord.*

John the Baptist:
A Message of Repentance
and of Spiritual Joy

The Master proclaimed you to be a prophet,
Higher than all the prophets
And greater than any man born of a woman.
For the One whom the prophets and the Law foretold,
You beheld him in your very flesh,
He, who is truly the Christ.
And you were more honored than all,
For you were chosen to baptize him.

FEAST OF THE SYNAXIS OF SAINT JOHN THE BAPTIST

An outstanding figure of the Advent drama is the precursor, John the Baptist. Throughout the season, the various Gospels read in church constantly remind us of his presence. Often we hear his strong message, urging us to prepare the way of the Lord. We also hear the words of Jesus: "What did you go out to the desert to see?...A prophet?...I am sending my messenger ahead of you; he will prepare your way before you." The spirit and message of John the Baptist remains with us throughout the Christmas season until the culmination on the glorious feast of the Theophany, in which John plays an important role, second only to that of the Lord himself. The

Theophany feast commemorates the Lord's baptism by John as well as the first time the entire Trinity is revealed in the New Testament.

God sends John, his messenger, to highlight and call attention to the words of the prophet Isaiah: "All the ends of the earth can see the salvation of our God!" John the Baptist heralds the good news that the Savior, the Messiah, is among us, in our midst. He is Christ's precursor, and he is also the "friend of the Bridegroom." During the course of the year, the liturgy provides us several occasions to return to the person, message, and the very special role/ministry of John the Baptist. For example, his birth date in June and his decapitation in August are reminders beyond Advent of the unique role John played in the plan of salvation. Conversely, during the last days of Advent, what matters most to us is to pay close attention to his message of conversion and repentance, and also one of unsurpassing joy. It is through true conversion and humble repentance, John the forerunner continues to suggest to us, that we can "level out the hills and the valleys" in our hearts and thus prepare there a sacred place for the Lord. If we do this, following the words and example of the precursor, we too shall experience the exceeding joy granted to him while leaping in his mother's womb at the nearness of Christ's presence in Mary.

John the Baptist was later to say that he rejoiced then "with great joy upon hearing the Bridegroom's voice." He leapt for joy on that occasion, when hidden in his mother's womb, while overhearing Mary's greeting to his mother Elizabeth. Already at that particular encounter there seemed to have been a very special affinity between him and the Savior he would later baptize on that first Theophany day. From his pre-infancy days

John could not help but be overjoyed at the nearness of the Lord's presence. That joy was the one thing he lived for. Later on in life, he would be led to the desert to prepare the Lord's path, and there he would be filled with the Holy Spirit's joy as he humbly prepared himself for the task ahead. In the desert, he knew what true joy was all about as he anxiously lived for the day he would again see his Savior, the true source of his joy. From the moment of that first meeting with Christ while both still in their mothers' wombs to the culminating one in the Jordan where he plays the role of Christ's baptizer, he, the "Bridegroom's friend," continues to rejoice with exceeding joy "because of the Bridegroom's voice."

John the Baptist is an exemplar of the ways of conversion and repentance and also an exemplar of the experience of true spiritual joy. In actuality there is no rivalry or opposition between these two—rather a deep, natural link. During these blessed Advent days, we must ask John the Baptist, our model and intercessor, to obtain for us both graces: the embracing on our part of sincere repentance and the gift of true inner joy. John the Baptist's unique mission was to bear witness to Christ—"he was not the Light, but came to testify to the Light"—and to point to him, the Lamb of God. Our mission, too, is (and this should be the source of our own joy) to remain close to Christ at all times and to continue showing him to the world daily by the quiet witness of our Christian lives.

> *Glorious John the Baptist,*
> *You heard the Father's voice from heaven testifying*
>   *to his Son,*
> *And you saw the Holy Spirit in the form of a dove*
> *Descending with the Father's words onto the*
>   *baptized One.*
> *O higher than all the prophets,*
> *Do not cease to intercede for us*
> *Who honor your memory with faith and love.*
>
> HYMN FOR THE SYNAXIS OF JOHN THE BAPTIST

Christmas Greetings

I wish you the joy of Christmas
The Holy Spirit's sweet repose,
I wish you the peace of Christmas
To make the old year's close;
I wish you the hope of Christmas
To cheer you on your way.
And a heart of faith and gladness
To face each coming day.

AUTHOR UNKNOWN

The angel said to them, "Do not be afraid; for behold,
I proclaim to you good news of great joy that will
be for all the people."

LUKE 2:10

There is a concrete moment in our Advent/Christmas journey that no matter what, it remains clear, almost vivid in my memory year after year. To some, it may seem totally irrelevant, insignificant, pointless. However, to a monk who labors under the weight of timeless monastic traditions, it is indeed a labor, and at that, a labor of love. I am referring to the time one yearly sits down to address countless season's greetings to our friends, families, volunteers, and to other monasteries. I tend to do this, usually, around the last week of Advent, when the Gospel readings speak of the Angel Gabriel being sent to Mary bearing tidings of good news. In the Gospel reading, the Archangel Gabriel is described as being sent from above, bringing greetings and good news to a humble maiden from Nazareth. In meditating this particular Gospel, and concretely on the mystery of the annunciation, I pause to reflect on the meaning of the word "send."

That word seems to carry a heavy weight of meaning. The word "send" is often taken for granted, but as I prepare our mailing and work its details I know full well that it will all end up being "sent" to many destinations, places, and an endless variety of recipients. The mind boggles at the endless possibilities of the traveling and its reception. At the end, all I can do is pray that our humble greetings, like that of Gabriel to Mary, bring comfort and joy to all those to whom the greetings are addressed.

On a very cold late-fall afternoon, it is a soothing and rewarding experience to sit down in front of a wood-burning stove, receiving a warm feeling from the blaze and hearing the crackling sound emanating from the fire as one begins to address endless amounts of envelopes. And as one continues with the labor of writing greetings and addressing envelopes, one can't help but notice the joy and coziness, almost the luxury, of doing a tedious task in front of a blazing, inviting, and comforting fire. Some monasteries keep the old tradition of sending their monastic chronicles as a form of Christmas newsletter. Written as such, it is usually a short account, plain and simple, of the news and events that have transpired in the monastery during the past year. These short messages tend to be rather didactic and to the point. Normally, monastics avoid newsy recaps of accomplishments or any other type of self-glorification that are neither monastic in spirit or style.

The work of letter writing at Christmastime is very special, and certainly, a concrete sign of our deep affection for others. The celebration of Christ's birth gives us the occasion to personally keep in touch with our families, our friends, our volunteers, our benefactors, and especially with the elderly and those in a more vulnerable life stage. To many of them, even the smallest expression of friendship is of significant value. Christmas, after all, is the celebration of God's love and charity for the world, for each and all of his children. The simple act of greeting one another at this time of the year, be it through writing, a phone call, or even a short email, is a concrete way of sharing in God's love and making it palpable to one another. For the believer, the mystery of Christmas increases the awareness that all ultimate reality consists in this: "God is love, and whoever remains in love remains in God and God in him" (1 John 4:16).

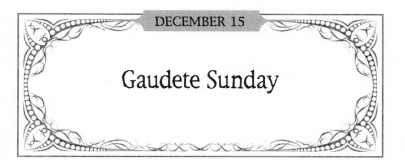

Gaudete Sunday

Rejoice in the Lord always! I shall say it again: rejoice! Your kindness should be known to all. The Lord is near.

PHILIPPIANS 4:4–5

As we move forward on our Advent pilgrimage, we reach the third Sunday of Advent, or Gaudete Sunday as it is commonly called in monasteries. The name "Gaudete" comes from the opening words of the Introit, which is sung at Mass: "*Gaudete in Domino, semper gaudete,*" which means, "Rejoice in the Lord always, again I say, rejoice." Joy is the theme of the entire liturgy for this particular Sunday. All its details, the texts, the music, the vestment worn by the celebrant, speaks of pure Advent joy. The clear message for this Sunday is the invitation to us Christians to rejoice, for the Lord is near. As we walk our Advent journey, we can almost see Christmas in the distance. As one of the lovely Office antiphons this week proclaims: "The Lord is coming and he shall not delay."

One more detail unique to Gaudete Sunday is the lighting in the evening of the pink candle in the Advent wreath. During the preceding weeks of the season, we have been waiting for the special moment. Indeed today is the day we light that unique candle in the wreath. I say unique, for of the four candles, it is the one different in color. The pink or rose color matches the color of the liturgical vestments for the day. The color symbolizes the joyous theme of the day.

Gaudete Sunday speaks to us of the proximity of the Lord's arrival. The Lord is now truly near, and that is the reason for our joy. The knowledge and almost palpable experience that the Lord is close at hand revitalizes our inner beliefs and encourages us all to give our undivided attention to the person of Jesus Christ, the God-made-man. The Incarnation of the Son of God is the source of our joy, for Christ comes to liberate us from the darkness, from a sinful state, and to introduce us to his Father. In welcoming Christ totally into our lives, we accept the salvation, freedom, and divine love he brings with his coming into the world. As we prepare with deep joy to discover his infant face at Christmas, we experience the joy that our Lady once felt when she embraced him in her arms for the first time. On Christmas Day, as we receive him in the Eucharist, it is he who shall come to embrace personally each of us, he the author and creator of our joy. "*Gaude et laetare semper in Domino, filia Sion.*"

> *Beautiful Savior, King of Creation,*
> *Son of God and Son of Man!*
> *Truly I'd love Thee,*
> *Truly I'd serve Thee.*
> *Light of my soul.*
> *My Joy, my Crown!*
> ANONYMOUS 1677, LEIPZIG

The Annunciation

*The Angel Gabriel said to Mary in greeting; Hail,
    full of grace, the Lord is with you; blessed are you
    among women.*

ADVENT ANTIPHON

*Behold, the Virgin, as was said of old,
Has conceived in her womb
And has brought forth God as a man,
Yet she remains a virgin.
Being reconciled to God through her,
Let us poor sinners sing her praises,
For she is truly the Theotokos.*

BYZANTINE MATINS FOR THE NATIVITY

uring this blessed season, the liturgical readings never
cease to remind us that Advent and Christmas are all
about the mystery of the Incarnation—a mystery that
begins when Mary, after being greeted by Gabriel and left dumb-
founded by his message, utters her fiat in complete submission
to the plan of God.

Mary, of course, already knew the words of the prophet Isaiah: "For a child is born to us, a son is given to us; upon his shoulder dominion rests. They name him Wonder-Counselor, God-Hero, Father-Forever, Prince of Peace." What she never knew, until that point in history, is that she was eternally destined to bear Emmanuel, the Father's only Son. As one of the lovely antiphons of Advent tells us, "This is the good news the prophets foretold: The Savior will be born of the Virgin Mary."

Throughout the whole of Advent, the icon of the annunciation lies next to the *Lectionary* in our chapel. Several times a day, as we enter or leave the oratory, we offer it a profound homage and kiss it reverently. During the liturgy, candles are lit next to the icon and incense is offered. As we gaze upon the icon, we see Mary in deep prayer. Suddenly, she is visited by Gabriel, and in her profound humility she seems bewildered by his greeting. If Mary is startled by the vision of the angel, she is even more startled by his message: "Do not be afraid, Mary, for you have found favor with God. Behold, you will conceive in your womb and bear a son, and you shall name him Jesus."

"How can this be, since I have no relations with a man?" we can hear Mary asking the angel. She had promised God to remain a virgin; was God asking her to do otherwise? Gabriel answered Mary quickly, reassuring her that the gift of her virginity would remain untarnished: "The holy Spirit will come upon you, and the power of the most high will overshadow you. Therefore, the child to be born will be called holy, the Son of God."

Overwhelmed, Mary, a woman of deep faith, utters her fiat: "Behold, I am the handmaid of the Lord. May it be done to me according to your word." Her "yes," spoken softly in a humble home in the village of Nazareth, changed the course of history. Through her simple utterance, God's plans for the world begin to unfold, and the Son of God descends into the womb of Mary, uniting heaven and earth. At that precise moment, the Word is made flesh and dwells among us! *Ecce iam venit, plenitudo temporis, in quo misit Deus filium suum in terras.*

O Sapientia
(O Wisdom)

O Wisdom, O holy Word of God's mouth,
You govern all creation with your strong yet tender
care.
Come and teach us all the ways that lead to life.

VESPERS FOR DECEMBER 17

he cold December chill permeates the quiet monastery. It is the kind of chill that sometimes seeps into our very bones. One longs for the warmth of a cozy fireplace, for the comfort that heat can give. It is the hour of vespers, and the bells are ringing with special solemnity. Starting today, the monasteries around the world make their solemn entrance into the last week of preparation before Christmas. The text of the lovely Advent vespers hymn "*Conditor Alme Siderum* (Loving Creator of the Stars)" changes to "*Verbum Salutis* (Word of Salvation)," and more importantly, the first of the great O Antiphons, "*O Sapientia* (O Wisdom)," begins to be sung at the time of the Magnificat. These beautiful antiphons, pregnant with meaning, are true bearers of Advent hope and joy. In them, according to a French liturgist, the liturgy of Advent finds its fullness and plenitude. The O Antiphons are extremely significant to both the Advent and the monastic liturgy. The rich spiritual content of the antiphons is invaluable, starting with the one we solemnly sing today, which opens with:

O Wisdom, O holy Word of God's mouth.

The wisdom we call forth is the Word of God. The Word, according to Saint John, has existed from the beginning in God's bosom. "In the beginning was the Word, and the Word was with God, and the word was God,"

he writes. The antiphon takes us to that moment before time began, to the Father's eternal engendering of the Son, of he who has "gone forth from the mouth of the Most High." Here, at vespers, our evening celebration in song, we sing of that first night before the world was created, when the Word came forth from the mouth of the Father, full of splendor, mystery, and majesty. Psalm 110 beautifully describes that glorious eternal moment: "Yours is princely power from the day of your birth. In holy splendor before the daystar, like dew I begot you."

> *You govern all creation with your strong yet tender care.*

Saint Paul tells us in his Letter to the Colossians that "in him were created all things in heaven and on earth, the visible and the invisible." God is the Creator, and Jesus, his eternal Son, is the Lord and master of this created universe. The universe was created for him, who in turn would come one day to redeem it. This universe, and all of us within it, he tends to with loving care.

Come; and teach us all the ways that lead to life.

This *Veni* of the antiphon is the pleading of our Advent journey. All along the days of Advent we have been praying, "Come, Lord Jesus, come." Now, in these solemn final days, we intensify our cry and plea for redemption. Once more we beg him to come and teach us the ways that lead to life eternal. "*Veni, ad docendum nos viam prudentiae.*"

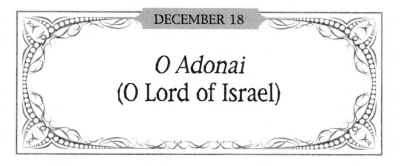

O Adonai
(O Lord of Israel)

O Lord and Giver of the Law on Sinai,
The Leader of your chosen people Israel,
Appearing in the burning bush,
Revealed to Moses face to face,
O come, stretch out your mighty arms to set us free.

VESPERS OF THE DAY

s we journey intensely into the final days of our Advent pilgrimage, we begin to feel more and more the exhilaration of knowing ourselves close to the arrival point. The majestic O Antiphons, full of poetic, symbolic richness, nurture our faith and expectation. They are our daily food on these last days, the theme that marks each day as we continue to climb the mountain of the Lord.

O Lord and Giver of the Law on Sinai.

Today we call forth the Savior with the invocation O *Adonai*, which in Hebrew translates to *El Shaddai*, the God who reveals himself to Moses on the mountain of Sinai. He is the God of the covenant and the ruler of the house of Israel. In contrast to those who may wish to deny the divinity of Christ, the faith of the ancient Church stands firm in its belief by calling the Savior with the name applied only to God in the Old Testament. The Church is telling us that Jesus, the "Anointed One of God" we await is, in the words of the Nicene Creed, "the Only Begotten Son of God, born of the Father before all ages. God from God, Light from Light, true God from true God." In truth he is the Messiah! With deep humility, we hold on to the ancient faith of the Church. Today, as in ages past, there will be those who contest it and wish to change it. There is no point in arguing with them, for

their minds are made up and their beliefs are already elsewhere. As Jesus said to the Samaritan woman, "If you knew the gift of God." Our faith is this gift of God, the faith preserved with deep integrity throughout the centuries, the faith that reveals Jesus as the only Son of God.

*Appearing in the burning bush, revealed to Moses
face to face.*

After Passover, the Lord leads his Chosen People through the desert for forty days and forty nights. It is after that long, arduous, and excruciating journey that God reveals himself to Moses in the burning bush. He not only reveals himself, but he also reveals his name. Like the Chosen People, we, too, are called to traverse the desert during our Advent journey, attempting to reach the mountain of the Lord, where he will reveal his name to us. The only difference now is that the name is a new one: Emmanuel. It is a new name to signify that he is about to forge a new covenant with his people.

O come, stretch out your mighty arms to set us free.

In the old covenant, the great sign of God's love for his people was made visible in their deliverance from Egypt and his leading them into the Promised Land. In the new covenant, his great love for us is not only manifested in his Incarnation and birth, which we are about to commemorate, but even more so during later years on Calvary when he "stretches out his mighty arms" on a wooden cross to save us. It is then that our true deliverance takes place, that our eternal freedom is gained. "*Veni ad redimendum nos in brachio extento.*"

> *O Adonai, faithful Shepherd of Israel,*
> *Come to us tonight during evening prayer*
> *As we invoke your holy name.*
> *Come and show us your face,*
> *A face full of tenderness and love.*

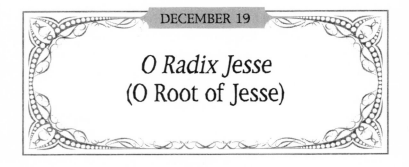

O Radix Jesse
(O Root of Jesse)

O Root of Jesse, sign of peace,
Before whom all nations stand in awe;
Kings stand silent in your presence;
The nations bow down in worship before You.
O come, and set us free;
Delay no longer in your love.

VESPERS OF THE DAY

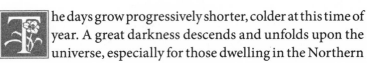

he days grow progressively shorter, colder at this time of year. A great darkness descends and unfolds upon the universe, especially for those dwelling in the Northern Hemisphere. Today at vespers, our evening song of praise, we are presented with another most powerful image of the one who is to come: *O Radix Jesse*, O Root of Jesse, or, in another translation, O Flower of Jesse's Stem. Once, the prophet Isaiah foresaw in a vision the destruction of Judah and the kingdom of David. The only remnant, Isaiah asserts, would be a humble root, a root from Jesse's stem: David's father. It is this humble root that would salvage David's lineage. From the stem of this root a Savior will bud and flower. The words from one of our most cherished Christmas carols express this in tender fashion:

Behold, a rose of Judah, from tender branch has
    sprung!
A rose from root of Jesse, as prophets long had sung.
It bore a flower bright
That blossomed in the winter
When half-spent was the night.
The rose of royal beauty of which Isaiah sings
Is Mary, maiden Mother, and Christ the flower
    she brings.
By God's unique design,
Remaining still a virgin,
She bore her Child divine.

The root of Jesse, in the words of the antiphon, is a sign of peace for all the people. Jesus, our Emmanuel, is sent by the Father to seal this new alliance of peace and reconciliation between the world and God: The Letter to the Colossians expresses this reality in a very precise manner:

> *"For in him all the fullness was pleased to dwell, and through him to reconcile all things for him, making peace by the blood of his cross (through him), whether those on earth or those in heaven."*
>
> COLOSSIANS 1:19–20

Jesus is the "Rex pacificus" we sing in the first antiphon of Christmas' first vespers, the Prince of Peace "whose face the whole world longs to see," as the antiphon attests. As he arrives on Christmas Day, a small and humble child, yet clothed in eternal splendor, all nations stand in awe. The world, in its long history, has never witnessed an event such as this!

*Kings stand silent in your presence; the nations bow
down in worship before you.*

This phrase from the antiphon not only anticipates Christmas but already gives us a glimpse into the solemnity of the Epiphany, when the Lord in all his glory shall be manifested to the gentiles. The Magi kings, coming from afar and seeing this glory shining in a small child, stand dumbstruck in awe in his presence, rapt in wonder and trepidation. As the Magi, we, too, stand immersed in deep silence before the great mystery. In this deep and reverent silence, we offer him our humble homage and adoration. "*Veni ad liberandum nos…*"

O come, and set us free; delay no longer in your love!

The plea *Veni ad liberandum nos*, or "come and deliver us," has been the cry of our hearts all along the Advent journey. Now that we see this salvation arriving so close at hand, we add the remaining supplication, "*Iam noli tardare* (come, Lord, and delay not)."

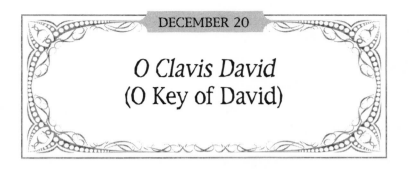

O Clavis David
(O Key of David)

O Key of David and Power of the house of Israel,
What you unlock, no man can close,
For you alone can bind fast.
O come, break down the prison walls of death
For those who dwell in darkness
And the shadow of death.

VESPERS OF THE DAY

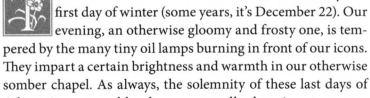

he calendar tells us that tomorrow is officially the first day of winter (some years, it's December 22). Our evening, an otherwise gloomy and frosty one, is tempered by the many tiny oil lamps burning in front of our icons. They impart a certain brightness and warmth in our otherwise somber chapel. As always, the solemnity of these last days of Advent is expressed by the many candles burning at vespers, including the oil lamps in front of our many icons, the incense used at the Lucernarium and the Magnificat, and the bells ringing joyously during the singing of the great O Antiphons and the Magnificat. The beauty of the Offices and the chant, the light and warmth from our candles, the sweet scent of the incense, the lovely sound of the bells: All of this changes what would usually be an ordinary winter evening into an expectant, festive nocturnal moment.

> *O Key of David and Power of the House of Israel.*

These are ancient messianic titles, used by the prophets to foretell the coming of the Messiah and designate his role. When Christ, the King of David, arrives, he will unlock and reveal all the secrets and mysteries of the old covenant. In him shall all the prophecies be fulfilled. In the new dispensation and covenant, he is head of a new Israel: the Church. He is the leader of this body, the family of the Church to which we all belong.

> *Therefore, he has power and dominion over us all.*
> *What you unlock, no man can close, for you alone*
>   *can bind fast.*

Christ, the Messiah, the Key of David, comes to unlock for all, Jews and gentiles alike, the doors of the kingdom of God. He alone possesses the keys and it will be he who invites all, be they just or sinners, into his eternal banquet. No one shall be excluded. This is precisely the good news of the Gospel he will proclaim one day.

> *O come, break down the prison walls of death, for*
> *those who dwell in darkness and the shadow of death.*

This is the fervent prayer of the expectant house of Israel, the cry for its liberation. *"Veni et educ vinctum de domo carceris…*(come and lead the prisoners from the prison house)." In Psalm 44 we find an echo of this sentiment which we, in turn, make our own:

Awake! Why do you sleep, O Lord?
Rise up! Do not reject us forever!
Why do you hide your face;
why forget our pain and misery?
For our soul has been humiliated in the dust;
our belly is pressed to the earth.
Rise up, help us!
Redeem us in your mercy.

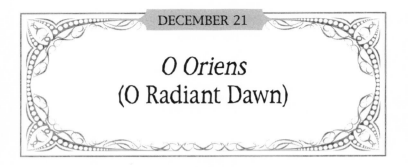

DECEMBER 21

O Oriens
(O Radiant Dawn)

O Daystar, splendor of eternal light
And Sun of Justice,
O come, shine on those who dwell in darkness
And the shadow of death.

VESPERS OF THE DAY

oday, in our hemisphere, the calendar marks the winter solstice. It is therefore the shortest day of the year. After the solstice, beginning on December 22, daylight slowly begins to lengthen. Similarly, we are at a point on our Advent journey in which we see the Light approaching at a close distance, the true Light who will shine on Christmas Day. This is the Light we have been seeking and have yearned for during the journey, the Light that will finally dispel all darkness from our hearts.

> *O Daystar, splendor of eternal light and Sun of*
> *Justice.*

The Latin *O Oriens* is translated in several different ways: O Daystar, O Dayspring, O Radiant Dawn. Each of these is rich in meaning and symbolic significance. In the early days of the

Church, the first Christian temples were constructed looking toward the east, *Ad orientem*, the Orient, from where Christ came and was expected to return. Our own oratory chapel is built that way, so that we can pray looking toward the east. The sun, a symbol of Christ, rises daily from the east. And from the sun, high in the heavens, comes light, heat, and life. Similarly it is from Christ, the Sun of Justice, that we Christians receive light, fire, and life. Christ, the Oriens from on high, is the Light of the World, and it is ultimately in his Light that we shall one day behold the radiance and splendor of the Father. "He who sees me sees the Father," proclaims Jesus. As we sing daily at vespers in the "*Phos Hilaron* (O Gladsome Light)":

> *O gladsome Light*
> *Of the Holy glory of the Immortal Father;*
> *Heavenly, holy, blessed Jesus Christ!*
>
> *O come, and shine on those who dwell in darkness*
> *and the shadow of death.*

It is because we are in a state of darkness, the darkness of our sinfulness and helplessness, that we recognize our instinctual need for light and salvation. Sinners that we all are, we recognize the deadly effects of sin in our lives. We know ourselves indeed sitting in a depressed, desperate state, under the "shadows of darkness and death." Christ alone can free us from these shadows. Fortunately for us, we know of his great love and compassion, his unbroken promise to come to us as our Savior. "*Veni et illumina sedentes in tenebris...*"

> *In the tender compassion of our God*
> *The dawn from on high shall break upon us,*
> *To shine on those who dwell in darkness and the*
> *   shadow of death*
> *And to guide our feet into the ways of peace.*

Or let us consider the words of the short old German hymn we sing daily during Advent:

> *Long is our winter, dark is our night;*
> *Come, set us free, O Saving Light!*

O Rex Gentium
(O King of the Nations)

O King of all nations,
The desired One of their hearts,
The cornerstone that joins in one
The people's sin had kept apart.
O come, and save the creature
You once formed from earth and dust.

VESPERS OF THE DAY

hold to the view that to benefit spiritually at a deeper level from the great O Antiphons, one has to learn to sing them in their original melody, either in Latin or in English. Fortunately there are wonderful and precise adaptations of English texts to the Gregorian melody. We know that in the Gregorian chant, the words and music are so tied together that to distill, syllable by syllable, the meaning of the words, we must make every effort to sing them. The exquisite Gregorian melody, used for all seven O Antiphons, is written in the same second mode, the "D mode," expresses beautifully the richness of the texts in all their evocation and complexity. This soul-stirring melody, one of the purest of the Gregorian repertoire, creates a soothing, healing, and serene effect in all those who sing or listen to it. The antiphons are a source of pure joy. For those who sing them, they become semi-sacramental, flowing like rivers through the body and mind, carrying us away in their currents.

As the psalmist says, "It is good to give thanks to the LORD, to sing praise to your name, Most High" (Psalm 92).

Those who cannot sing the antiphons in their original Gregorian melody can still use the text and sing them to the tune of "O Come, O Come, Emmanuel." This is very practical for home use around the table, at dinnertime. Those who cannot sing at all can pray it, listening if they can to a recorded rendition of the antiphons. Many of the Gregorian chant compact discs carry it.

O King of all nations, the desired One of their hearts

In the preceding O Antiphons, our point of reference was the Jewish Old Testament, using the messianic titles the Israelites applied to the expectant Messiah. Starting today, our horizon enlarges to encompass all peoples. The Messiah, the Savior sent by God, comes to be king not only of the Chosen People but of all peoples, including the gentile nations. As a matter of fact, a literal translation of *O Rex Gentium* would read, "O King of the gentiles." God, in his great love, calls all his children of the earth to salvation. He offers them, Jews and gentiles alike, a Savior. Jesus is sent by the Father into the world to unite all peoples and be king of all. In the words of Saint Paul, "There is neither

Jew nor Greek, there is neither slave nor free person, there is not male and female; for you are all one in Christ Jesus" (Galatians 3:28). The people's great longing for his coming, therefore, is not surprising. He is the "Desired One" of their hearts, for he is the one who has come to free them from their previous captivity. He is the one who comes to bring unity to all of his people.

> *The cornerstone that joins in one the people's sin had kept apart*

Jesus, in Matthew 21:42, calls himself the cornerstone, the foundation upon which his Church will be built. It is in this Church, his body, that he will gather all people into one. Those of all languages and nationalities, races and backgrounds, will finally find their true home in the one Church of God, whose cornerstone is Christ himself.

> *O come, and save the creature you once formed from earth and dust.*

Our Advent cry for help, "O come," is heard at the completion of the antiphon. "O come, and save the creature you once formed from the dust" is our plea to God's pity and love. We pray and never cease praying. Whether we need something or not, prayer is our one direct recourse to God. As a great saint once said, "Prayer is the one thing that touches the heart of God." In these last days of Advent we keep vigil in constant prayer that we may worthily receive the gift from on high: Christ, our Savior. "*Veni, salva hominem, quem de limo formasti.*"

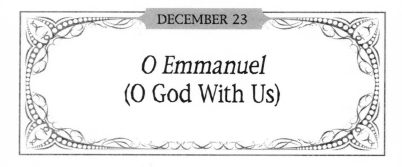

O Emmanuel
(O God With Us)

O Emmanuel, our King and Lawgiver,
The long-awaited hope of the nations,
Savior of all people;
O come, our Lord and God,
Set free the people whom You love.

VESPERS OF THE DAY

ow that our Advent journey is about to draw to a close, we turn our thoughts to Bethlehem. In spirit, we travel to that faraway place, where the great mystery is to be unveiled in a humble babe. A Byzantine liturgical text tells us:

Now that the time of our salvation draws near…
prepare yourself, O Bethlehem, for the birth. Receive
the Mother of God: for she comes to you to give birth
to the Light that never sets…Let everything that has
breath praise the Maker of all!

Tonight we praise the Lord with the last of our Advent vespers. The final of the great O Antiphons is sung. Already at lauds, during our morning praise, the liturgy forecasting the news told us to ready ourselves: *Ecce completa sunt*, we proclaimed, or, "Behold, all things are accomplished." This refers to those things spoken by the angel concerning the Virgin Mary. As the bells ring during the singing of the last O Antiphon and the Magnificat, we draw deeply into ourselves once more, knowing now with certainty that the prophecies of long ago are soon to be fulfilled.

O Emmanuel, our King and Lawgiver,
the long-awaited hope of nations

For the first time today we call upon the one who is coming with the name given to him by the angel: Emmanuel, meaning "God is with us." We recall also the words of the prophet Isaiah: "The young woman, pregnant and about to bear a son, shall name him Emmanuel." The very meaning of the name reveals to us the depth and tenderness of God's love for us. He wants to be one of us, to dwell and remain with us always. He desires to share our human nature, and he wants us to share his divine life. Indeed, he is the "lover of humankind," as the Eastern Liturgy frequently calls him. With his coming among us, we stand in awe as "the grace of God has appeared, saving all" (Titus 2:11). The long-awaited hope of all nations is soon to be rewarded and fulfilled.

O come, our Lord and God,
set free the people whom You love.

This last *Veni*, the final O come, summarizes our entire Advent journey: its prayer, longing, and constant yearning for salvation. Come, Lord, set free the people whom you love. This last verse of the antiphon gives us the necessary incentive we need for the last miles of our journey. A little bit longer, and then tomorrow his glory shall be revealed to us! "*Veni ad salvandum nos, Domine Deus noster.*"

Christmas Eve

> *What can I give him*
> *Poor as I am;*
> *If I were a shepherd,*
> *I would give him a lamb,*
> *If I were a wise man,*
> *I would do my part.*
> *But what can I give him?*
> *I will give him my heart.*
>
> MY GIFT, BY CHRISTINA G. ROSSETTI

hristmas Eve holds a distinctive status in the monastic calendar. In the days of old, December 24 was a day of strict fasting—a fast that could not be broken until after the completion of the first solemn vespers of the feast. Not even a piece of candy could be tasted or eaten. In later years, when the fast was dispensed, we could enjoy a small supper as a prelude to tomorrow's feast, a supper with enough nourishment to sustain us throughout the long night Offices and the midnight Mass.

On the morning of Christmas Eve, during the hour of Prime, the abbot, vested in the appropriate ornaments, with two candle bearers and a monk carrying the incense, sings solemnly the august proclamation or announcement of the Nativity. It is an incomparable moment. The proclamation begins with the fixation of the date according to ancient counting. Then the announcement continues with these words:

> *In this era of the world's history*
> *Jesus Christ, eternal God and Son of the*
>   *Eternal Father,*
> *desires to save the world by his gracious coming.*
> *He was conceived by the Holy Spirit,*
> *and now after nine months …*
> (at this point the monks kneel)
> *He is born at Bethlehem in the Tribe of Judah*
> *as Man from the Virgin Mary …*
> (The monks lay prostrate and touch their foreheads
>   to the ground)
> *This is how it took place,*
> *the birth of our Lord Jesus Christ in the flesh.*

The profound prostration of the monks at that precise moment expresses the totality of their humble adoration before God's great mystery. After the solemn proclamation of the feast of the Incarnation is concluded, the remaining of the martyrology is read until its usual ending. Then the abbot gives a brief homily and offers his first Christmas greeting to the monastic community. One by one, the monks offer the abbot and each other the kiss of peace and their warmest Christmas wishes. The whole monastery, though immersed in the early-morning stillness, begins to show signs of joyful anticipation.

The rest of the monastic day, until the time for the first vespers, is spent as in every other Christian household: making final preparations for the arrival of the Lord, decorating the tree, placing the last touches on the crèches around the monastery, final cleaning, choir practice, preparing the food for the *réveillon* (Christmas post-midnight celebration) and for Christmas Day itself. It is a busy series of moments in an otherwise quiet and ordinary monastic day. As much as possible, one tries to temper the business by holding on to the quiet and reflective

spirit cultivated throughout Advent. After all, the great event we are about to celebrate, the birth of Jesus, must occur—before anyplace else—in the quiet and innermost spaces of our hearts.

The danger we all face, especially in the last days before Christmas, is to allow ourselves to be taken up with the bustling activities of the season. The gifts, parties, and other such things reduce our attention from the focal point of our celebration, the arrival of Christ on this holy night. It may be almost impossible to avoid the so-called "Christmas rush" altogether; however, with a bit of creativity and a sense of priorities, we can limit its influence by making room for deeper silence in our lives, and by taking time for quiet prayer.

The first two antiphons of today's vespers, the first vespers of the Solemnity, address the Savior as the King of Peace. He comes to each of us personally and to the whole world at large, as our king bearing his gift of peace. He makes his face shine upon us, and with his shimmering radiance, he saves us.

> *Far, far away is Bethlehem,*
> *And years are long and dim,*
> *Since Mary held the Holy Child*
> *And angels sang for him.*
> *But still to hearts where love and faith*
> *Make room for Christ in them,*
> *He comes again, the Child from God,*
> *To find his Bethlehem.*

W. RUSSELL BOWLE

The Lord's Genealogy: The Solemn Proclamation of Christ's Birth

Come, O faithful and let us celebrate in song
the ensemble of the Lord's ancestors:
Adam, the first-born, Enoch, Noah,
Melchisedech, Abraham, Isaac and Jacob.
And after the Law was given, Moses and Aaron,
Joshua, Samuel and David
and with them also Isaiah, Jeremiah, Ezekiel, Daniel,
and the twelve prophets without forgetting Elijah,
        Eliseus
and all the other holy fathers.
Let us then remember Zachariah and John the Baptist
and all those who shall announce the coming of Christ,
our Life and Resurrection,
and who alone grants eternal life to humankind.

BYZANTINE *APOSTICHA* (HYMN)
FOR SUNDAY OF THE HOLY ANCESTORS OF CHRIST

t is an ancient custom in monasteries that in the early morning after singing the morning Office, the monks would usually gather together in the chapter room to receive their work assignments for the day. Normally, where this is possible, the monks go in procession from the monastic oratory to the chapter room. Once gathered in that room, a capitulation or short chapter from the Rule of Saint Benedict, is read. (The "chapter" room name originates from this custom.) After the Rule, the martyrology is read; this is where the feast days and saints celebrated in the following day are announced. This in itself is very important because, in accordance with monastic usage, liturgical celebrations start in the eve with the singing of vespers, at the time of the sun's setting. The language used in the martyrology is rather unique, antique in quality, and it has its own archaic rhythms. It usually contains a certain short eulogy of the saints mentioned. After the reading, there is typically a brief exhortation by the abbot, and then the distribution of work for the day is given. Finally, a simple prayer is said to bless the work of the day.

It is in this context of the monastic day that the solemn Christmas proclamation is made on the morning of December 24. (Some monasteries and churches prefer to do this at night before their midnight Mass.) The reader is accompanied to the center of the room, where a decorated page from the martyrology rests on the reading stand. He is accompanied by two candle bearers and another monk bearing incense. Surrounded by the other monks, after incensing the selected page, the reader or celebrant begins to sing the solemn Christmas proclamation. At the words "in Bethlehem of Judea," he stops for a moment and everyone kneels down, prostrate in silent adoration, touching their foreheads to the floor. It is a rare and most touching moment in the monastic liturgy, which allows us to recall the birth of Jesus in the context of salvation history.

Into our world, after a long history measured in centuries of the human experience, with all its ups and downs, today enters a Savior, bringing us a promise of salvation. There are several translations of this solemn proclamation. The following one, translated from the French and in usage in some of France's monasteries, is an accepted one for liturgical usage:

> Be with us, Lord, Father most holy, be with us, eternal and all-powerful God, you who have spoken to our fathers through the prophets. Be with us, Lord, today. Unknown ages from the time you created heaven and earth and then formed Adam and Eve in your own image. After the first sin, you promised them a Savior. Twenty-one centuries from the time you called Abraham and Sarah, who believed in your promise, you then chose their descendants, Isaac, Jacob, and the tribe of Judah. Thirteen centuries after Moses led Israel's people out of Egypt, thus sealing an alliance with them. Eleven hundred years from the time of Ruth and the prophets, 1,000 years from

the anointing of David as King. You loved Israel with an eternal love, thus bestowing your favor upon it. When the hearts of the poor were ready, to those who awaited the consolation of Israel you sent a man whose name was John to prepare the way for the Lord by making straight the path for him. When the times were fulfilled, and in fullness on the 752nd year from the foundation of Rome on the forty-second year of the reign of Emperor Augustus, the whole world being in a peaceful state, in Bethlehem of Judea was born from the Virgin Mary, Jesus Christ, your eternal Son, God made flesh, conceived by the Holy Spirit making his appearance in our world nine months later as Emmanuel, "God with us."

Eternal God and Son of the eternal Father, who wished to sanctify the world by his merciful coming—therefore, heavenly Father, we your humble servants together with the angels and archangels and the whole of creation wish to keep vigil on this holy night, to sing your love and to proclaim your mercy. For yours is the kingdom, the power, and the glory forever and ever. Amen.

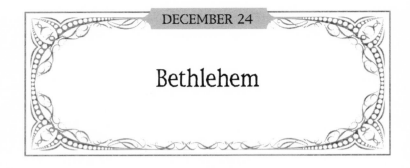

Bethlehem

Be glad and rejoice, O Bethlehem
Land of Judea.
For from you the Lord shines forth as the dawn.
Give ear, you mountains and hills,
And all lands surrounding Judea.
For Christ is coming to save the people
Whom he has created and whom he loves.

BYZANTINE VESPERS, SUNDAY BEFORE THE NATIVITY

Bethlehem in Judah's land, how glorious your future!
The King who will rule my people comes from you.

LAUDS, ANTIPHON FOR DECEMBER 24

Let us again and again make our way to Bethlehem
and gaze upon this Word made Flesh by Almighty
God who has become a little One. In this visible
Word cut short we may learn the wisdom of God
which has become humility.

BLESSED GUERRIC D'IGNY, FIFTH CHRISTMAS SERMON

The people of Israel survived the tribulations of the centuries because they continued, no matter what, to hope and hold to God's promise. They believed in the partnership, a special pact, the alliance that God once made with them. Throughout the centuries they listened to the prophets who spoke to them God's word and who reminded them of this promise. The prophets announced repeatedly to Israel's people that the Lord would send them, perhaps soon, a liberator, a Savior, a Messiah. The pious people of ancient Israel believed in God's promise and so they waited patiently for the arrival of God's Anointed One. From the prophet Micah they learned that the Messiah, like David his ancestor, would one day be born in the tiny town of Bethlehem. We shall not be surprised about this, for the Almighty always makes use of the smallest, humblest, and most obscure places to reveal himself. As we approach Christmas, it is time for our own personal journey into Bethlehem. In one of the beautiful Byzantine antiphons of the prefeast of the Nativity we read:

"Let us celebrate, O you people, the forefeast of the Nativity of Christ, raising our minds on high, let us in spirit go to Bethlehem and with our inner eyes let us look at the Mother-to-be as she hastens to the cave to give birth to our God, the Lord of all. Joseph, when he beheld the marvel of this wonder, thought that he saw a mortal wrapped as a babe in swaddling clothes; but from all that came to pass he understood that he was the true God, who alone grants great mercy. Let us, indeed, raise our minds on high and in spirit journey to Bethlehem to contemplate the great mystery in the cave. For paradise is open once again when, from a pure Virgin, God comes forth perfect in his divinity as in his humanity."

Today, in our times, Bethlehem is not just a village in the Middle East. For us, disciples and followers of Jesus, Bethlehem is a spiritual condition of mind and heart in which we are all invited to abide, for it is there, in the very depths of our hearts that Christ wishes to be born today. *"Hodie Christus natus est nobis!* (Christ has been born for us today!)"

The center of our hearts is the very cave in which Jesus wishes to be born today. It is our hearts, therefore, that we must eagerly prepare to welcome him and as the place for his dwelling. Again, the haunting *troparion* (hymn) for the prefeast of the Nativity as it sings, it also inspires us with its most tender, powerful words:

> *Prepare, O Bethlehem,*
> *For Paradise has been open to all.*
> *Adorn yourself, O Ephrata,*
> *For the Tree of life blossoms forth*
> *From the Virgin in the cave.*
> *Her womb is a spiritual paradise*
> *Planted with the divine fruit;*
> *If we eat of it, we shall live forever*
> *And not die like Adam.*

For Christ comes to restore the image
Which he created from the beginning.

Similarly, on Christmas Day, when Christ is born in our innermost, the tree giving new life shall be planted deep within the cave of our hearts. By the grace of the Holy Spirit, we are invited to partake of its fruit and rejoice in the fullness of life being offered to us as it was once to Mary, the true God-bearer who carried him in her blessed womb for nine long months.

> *Make ready in haste, O Bethlehem,*
> *for Paradise is opened...*
> *Salvation enters the world and the curse destroyed.*
> *Prepare, make ready, O hearts of righteous people,*
> *Instead of myrrh, bring songs as a wise offering.*
> *Receive, therefore, salvation and immortality*
> *For both your bodies and souls.*
> *Behold the Master arrives to lay in a manger*
> *And he urges us to complete our spiritual songs.*
> *Let us praise him without ceasing:*
> *O Lord, Glory to You!*

A modern writer aptly describes the transcendent role tiny Bethlehem played in the overall divine plan:

> *Christ was born in the first century, yet he belongs*
> *to all centuries.*
> *He was born a Jew, yet he belongs to all races*
> *He was born in Bethlehem, yet he belongs*
> *to all places and countries.*
>
> GEORGE W. TRUETT

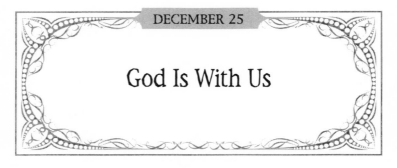

God Is With Us

God is with us!
Understand, all you nations.
And submit yourselves
For God is with us!
BYZANTINE CHRISTMAS ANTHEM

ur Christmas liturgical celebration officially begins with the singing of the first vespers of the Nativity on the early evening of December 24, Christmas Eve. As we process into the chapel and venerate the beautiful Nativity icon, we hasten to celebrate in song the Lord's arrival in our midst. Our chanting begins with the customary blessing for solemn feasts: "Glory to the Holy, Consubstantial, and Undivided Trinity, etc." Immediately after, we intone and sing three times the short Byzantine anthem that presides over all our monastic Offices during the Christmas season:

God is with us, God is with us!
Understand all you nations.
And submit yourselves,
And submit yourselves
For God is with us!

These initial lines found in the Book of Isaiah are chanted and repeated over and over in our Offices. They remind us profoundly of the true meaning of Christmas: the Lord has arrived and entered our world, he is now truly Emmanuel, God with us! Isaiah's prophecy is today fulfilled! God's promise to his people becomes today a permanent reality. As we sing and repeat the short anthem we proclaim our faith in the mystery that God is indeed with us, that the Word became flesh to become Emmanuel, to dwell among us. Isaiah's prophetic word is plain and clear in its solemn proclamation:

> *For a child is born to us, a son is given to us;*
> *upon his shoulder dominion rests.*
> *They name him Wonder-Counselor, God-Hero,*
> *Father-Forever, Prince of Peace.*
> *His dominion is vast*
> *and forever peaceful.*
>
> ISAIAH 9:5–6

On Christmas Day, on the very depths and mystery of the holy night, Emmanuel, the Christ Child, is born unto us. God appears on earth, and he is in truth one with us. All peoples of the earth are called to acknowledge that he, Emmanuel, is indeed the Messiah, the Anointed One of God, and therefore, all of us must submit to him. Christ-Emmanuel is the Light of the World, and he comes to free us from the darkness we are engulfed in. He comes to make us free and to share his very life with us. We submit to him in complete freedom and joy, for in his infinite love he came to save us, to be one with us!

Christmas:
The Holy Night

The door is on the latch tonight,
The hearth-fire is aglow;
I seem to hear the passing feet—
The Christ Child in the snow.
My heart is open wide tonight,
For stranger, kith, or kin:
I would not bar a single door
Where love might enter in.

ON CHRISTMAS EVE, AUTHOR UNKNOWN

O Holy Night! The stars are brightly shining.
It is the night of the dear Savior's birth;
Long lay the world in sin and error pining.
Till he appeared and the soul felt its worth.

CANTIQUE DE NOEL, OLD FRENCH CAROL

s we reach the final hours of Christmas Eve, we feel a great sense of relief and anticipation, for we at last see the culmination of our Advent journey: the Lord is at the door and knocking, and we are eager to greet and welcome him in. This has been the sole purpose of the austere long journey, and now the mystery is to be revealed to us, to the whole world, in all its heavenly splendor. Our celebrations started earlier in the day with the singing of the solemn announcement of the Nativity, and as we move on, we proceed with the singing of the solemn first Christmas vespers. After the intonation of the "God is with us" for the first time in this glorious season, we continue with the ancient, beautiful, poetic hymn sung at vespers services during Christmastide: *"Jesu Redemptor Omnium* (Jesus Redeemer of the World)." From the first stanza of the hymn we are transported to another realm, to that eternal night when the Word is mysteriously begotten in the bosom of the immortal Father before the ages began. The text of the hymn is a reminder that today's commemoration has its origins in that timeless, divine beginning. As we proceed with the hymn, we are brought back to earth to the very event that is the purpose of our celebration: the Nativity in the flesh of Jesus, the Christ, the Father's only eternal Son. The hymn's Gregorian melody is so lovely and sober, the verses are filled with such unction, that I think it is appropriate to quote some of them here:

> *This is the great day of the year*
> *When Christians join to celebrate*
> *Your coming down to save humankind,*
> *The Father's glory lay aside.*
> *The earth, the sky, the very sea,*
> *And all that live in them, rejoice,*
> *And praise the Father who decreed*
> *That you should come to us in human form.*

Our faith opens our inner eyes to the wonder of the Christmas mystery. Faith tells us that what we celebrate and proclaim at

Christmas is this marvelous exchange sung in the antiphon "*O Admirabile Commercium* (O Wonderful Exchange)," the nuptials, so to speak, of divinity from on high with our poor sinful humanity here below. This wedding, this unique transformation we describe as the Incarnation, is accomplished in the person of Jesus, the sweet and humble infant from the crèche. This tiny infant is the wondrous link that unites heaven and earth. He is the very center of our human history, the only reason for which the world exists. All creation, us included, was made by him and for him; therefore everything in the universe looks to him for life, salvation, and final redemption. Tonight, the mystery that unfolds before our very eyes is his birth from a humble Virgin, in a desolate cave in tiny Bethlehem, to accomplish the work of our salvation. O wondrous mystery! As the Magnificat vespers antiphon sings:

> *Today, Christ the Lord is born;*
> *Today, the Savior has appeared.*
> *Today, the angels sing on earth,*
> *And the archangels rejoice!*
> *Today all the just exult proclaiming:*
> *Glory to God in the highest, Alleluia.*

The summit of our Christmas festivities reaches its endpoint with the celebration of the Divine Liturgy precisely at midnight, (though this has changed a bit throughout the years and is now sometimes anticipated during earlier night hours). I call this the summit of our Christmas Day because it is the moment when the Savior, the small Bethlehem infant, comes to be born in each of us through the sacrament of the holy Eucharist. As usual, there is a great deal of rich symbolism in the liturgy, particularly in a one celebrated in the middle of a dark winter night, the holiest of nights. One of the ancient Christmas liturgical texts, *Dum medium silentium* (while all things were in quiet silence), describes its reason better than any of us could: "While all things were in deep silence, and the night was in the midst of her course, your almighty Word leapt down from heaven, from your royal throne, O Lord." Indeed, our celebration of the holy night is an intangible symbol, both of that eternal moment, the night when the

Word was engendered and came forth from the Father, and the night of time and history, when the same Word becomes flesh and appears before our eyes for the first time in Bethlehem: *Et Verbum caro factum est et habitavit in nobis!* (The Word was made flesh and dwelled among us.)

There is another reason, another compelling symbol, for our keeping prayerful vigil during the incipient hours of the holy night. If we await a Savior's coming during the darkest hours of night, it is because of our own experience with the dark forces of evil and thus our longing to be liberated from them with the arrival of the Light. Our hearts and minds, plunged as they are in the obscurity of sin and despair, instinctively know Christ alone is the true Light, the "Light from Light" ("*Lumine de Lumine*"), the Light of the World. In the depths and anguish of our own personal night, the mystery of Christmas comes as liberation at the very center of our lives. As we traverse the darkness, we are no longer alone, for our incarnate Lord comes to console us, to be near us, to save us. And as he comes, he brings us the promise of his light, his love, his peace, so that all may be well with us and our loved ones. On this holy night, as we keep vigil in the company of our Lady and Saint Joseph, with the angelic choirs of heaven and the simple shepherds on earth, let us express our gratitude to the Father for his most precious gift to us on this holiest of nights: our Lord Jesus Christ, the Savior of the world!

> *At your first coming to us, O Christ,*
> *Your will was to save the children of Adam's race;*
> *When you come again to judge us,*
> *Show mercy to those who honor today*
> *your holy Nativity!*

CANON FROM THE PREFEAST OF THE NATIVITY

DECEMBER 26

A Joyful Season

The joy of brightening each others' lives,
Bearing each others' burdens, easing each others'
loads
And supplanting empty hearts and lives
With generous gifts becomes for us
The magic of Christmas.

W.C. JONES

For at the moment the sound of your greeting reached
my ears, the infant in my womb leaped for joy.

LUKE 1:44

hristmastide is a special season for joy. The Lord is born, he is in our midst, and as true disciples we enjoy the gift of his company. There are many personal ways by which each of us can contribute to make this holy season joyful, brighter, and filled with meaning. Some of the suggestions here simply are quiet reminders of how to go about keeping the Christmas spirit alive in the depths of our hearts, and from there, to go out to others and share the good tidings with them. These ideas, of course, are meant to be adapted to each individual circumstance:

1. In the midst of a very hectic and agitated season, it is wise to take time out for quiet prayer and contemplation. Be it in the early morning, in the middle of the day, or sometime in the evening, we can withdraw apart into moments of stillness and share some time alone with the Lord. This will allow God to speak directly to our hearts and our hearts to him. There is nothing like a quiet moment of silence and prayer to anchor us more deeply in God's presence.

2. Keep at all times a joyful attitude, a cheerful disposition. The Book of Proverbs asserts that a cheerful disposition is always good for our health (Proverbs 17:22). Very often, behind all the Christmas festivities, one notices a high level of sadness and depression, and deep feelings of loneliness. Inspired by faith, we can use the holy season to find joy in God's pres-

ence and to bring this to others. Joy is contagious, and we should all share a joyful attitude with those who surround us. Sooner or later, our friends and families will discover that this cheerful attitude is rooted in our union with God.

3. Let us make a point of practicing patience, kindness, generosity, and thoughtfulness toward one another, and especially toward the poor. These are traits of true disciples of Jesus, and they can bring peace and acceptance to all those who suffer, struggle, are all alone, or are undergoing pain. Our care and genuine concern for the welfare of others is an authentic sign of Christian love, of being faithful to the Lord's teaching: "Bear one another's burdens." For instance, a simple visit to someone who is alone, sick, or elderly can relieve the painful solitude of that person and add a touch of joy to his or her day.

4. At all times let's keep a peaceful heart. Instead of plunging ourselves into the noise, the abundance, and commercialization of the season, let us inwardly cultivate a quiet and peaceful heart. We can only find peace and calmness within the confines of our own selves. Inner peace is a gift from the Lord. Let us beseech him day and night for his gift. And let us help him by cultivating actively all those things that lead to inner peace. Like the angels on that first Christmas night, let us pray and work for peace on earth.

5. Let us nurture our souls with good reading about different aspects of this holy season. We can start by reading daily the Gospel accounts of the Nativity and meditating upon them. We can also read about Christmas legends, stories, and rich

traditions, particularly those of other countries. There are some beautiful, touching stories connected with Christmas. Let us also refresh and nurture our intellect with Christmas poetry, inspirational seasonal writing, Christmas letters, meditations, and sermons of old, such as the ones from the Fathers, always appropriate for this time of the year.

6. Spend quality time in front of the Nativity scene, the crèche. Study carefully the expression of all those personages or figurines that are part of the crèche, especially the Baby Jesus, his Mother, and Saint Joseph. Allow yourself to be carried away by a sense of wonder and thanksgiving, as did the humble shepherds and the Magi at the sight of Jesus. The Nativity scene displayed in each Christian home is a source of grace, joy, and beauty to all those who dwell in that house. In Europe the crèche is kept in homes usually until February 2, the feast of the Lord's Presentation and the fortieth day after Christmas. A day of completion!

7. Be faithful to the traditions passed on from one generation to another in your family, parish, school, or circle of friends. At the same time never be afraid to create new and timely Christmas traditions for now and the future. New traditions open us to new possibilities and allow us to remain open to the Lord's designs. And while we do this, let us remember fondly our memories from the past, those treasured Christmas memories we keep in the depths of our hearts, and be grateful to God for them.

8. Take time to enjoy the small details of the holidays by visiting different places that inspire Christmas cheer. Admire the

beauty and variety of Christmas trees in the village green and in your surroundings, and take in the lovely Christmas lights. The glow from these lights dispels the gloom of our long, dark, winter nights. Visit some of the local houses open to the public and decorated for the occasion. Be sure to bring some newly picked holiday greens and fresh herbs to cheer your home with their fragrance and loveliness. Deck the halls whenever possible. Enjoy the pleasures and warmth of a cozy fire at home. There is nothing more comforting to our spirits than sharing quality time with friends and family in front of a crackling fire at home. Celebrate the present moment.

9. Remember the place and ritual of prayer and grace at home. Use special Christmas prayers or even sing a Christmas carol together before you start your daily meals. It invokes God's blessings and brings the joy of the season to all those who partake of your table. If you live near a monastery, try to attend the vespers service whenever possible. The liturgy of Christmas is very rich and powerful, and it continues to be celebrated throughout all the days of the season, all the way to the feast of the Theophany or baptism of the Lord.

10. Make your gift exchanges simple and meaningful. Give from the heart, and, whenever possible, give homemade simple gifts. Homemade gifts are particularly appreciated, for they are made with love and creativity, and this often shows. There is no point in wasting resources on expensive gifts. The humble shepherds of the crèche brought their lambs to the Infant Jesus. It was all they had, all they could give besides the love in their hearts.

11. Enjoy the music of the season and make often a joyful noise unto the Lord with your own singing of the sounds of Christmas. Continue, if you like, to listen to Handel's *Messiah*, the many oratorios and Christmas cantatas, especially Bach's famous *Christmas Oratorio*. It is gorgeous music, it feeds the soul. Listen to the music of Corelli, especially his concerti for *La Notte di Natale*, music of Telemann, Vivaldi, and others. All are inspiring, soothing, and beautiful. Enjoy the tenderness and intimacy of the Christmas carols. Again and again they recall the Christmas miracle.

12. Love is the essence and true spirit of Christmas. Christmas has its origins in God's love for us. The Father sent his only Son into the world out of his immense love for each of us. Our Lady welcomed him into her arms with love. We must likewise honor the spirit of Christmas by abiding in the love the Holy Spirit himself poured into our hearts. Christmas gives us the occasion to rediscover the nature of true love and to love more creatively. We must daily grow in love for God and for one another. Let God's love take over our hearts so completely that it becomes clearly manifested in the way we love and treat others.

Two Christmas Traditions: The Crèche and the Icon of the Nativity

While they were there, the time came for her to have her child, and she gave birth to her firstborn son. She wrapped him in swaddling clothes and laid him in a manger, because there was no room for them in the inn.

LUKE 2:6–7

For Christ is born and born again,
When his love lives in the hearts of men.

W.D. DARRITY

The hinge of history is on the door of a Bethlehem stable.

RALPH W. SOCKMAN

ne of the most beloved and enduring of our monastic Christmas traditions is the building and arranging of the crèche, the Nativity scene, which represents the story of the birth of Christ. The tradition of the crèche is not only popular in monasteries, schools, and churches, but it extends from the richest to the humblest of homes. A poignant and profound faith keeps alive this beautiful tradition in our homes year after year. This tender French word "crèche" or "crib" in English is commonly used to describe this ancient Christian custom. Nativity scenes come in all sizes. The diversity of Nativity sets, often handcrafted with cultural elements referencing the artist's background, is itself a witness to the universal acknowledgment of the mystery of the Incarnation.

There is a long tradition claiming that Saint Francis of Assisi re-created for the first time a live representation of the Nativity scene in the small town of Greccio, Italy. Saint Francis wished to portray for some of his often-illiterate fellow citizens a living reminder of the drama, charm, and beauty of the first Christmas. It is said that those in attendance at the midnight Mass, as they stood in front of the living crèche, broke down in tears of joy and deep emotion. Here in the monastery, we have several Nativity sets that are arranged and displayed in distinct monastic places: the chapel, the refectory, the library, and the parlor. A few days before Christmas, especially on the fourth Sunday of Advent, while a myriad of preparations are fervently undertaken around the monastery, we begin to erect the crèche in the chapel and in the common room, or parlor. We bring down the boxes from the attic and begin to unwrap the santons or figurines that are part of the Christmas scene.

In Provence, the children charmingly call this activity the "waking up of the santons from their deep sleep." As we keep sorting out the santons and slowly begin to arrange the crèche, I enjoy thinking about the universal nature of the custom and cherish the thought that other monasteries and people in other lands and cultures are preparing to do the same. At this time, it is comforting to think that no matter what barriers of culture or language may separate us, we are all united in the one faith, in a common yearning for the arrival of the Savior. We slowly build the "Bethlehem" landscape of fields and hills and place the stable where it belongs. With great reverence and tenderness we begin placing the statue of our Lady and Saint Joseph in the stable or cave, depending on the particular year's arrangement. We do not place the *Petit* Jesus statue until just before the first vespers of the feast is sung. He arrives just in time for the celebration! The other santons are arranged around the stable, especially the shepherds and the sheep, for in truth they represent our own little flock at the crèche. Other farm animals are also well-represented: cattle, donkeys, chickens, a rooster, ducks, dogs, and cats. The people of the surrounding village join as well if it is done in Provence. The figures of the three Magi are placed at a distance, for it is not yet time for their arrival. Once the crèche is fully mounted we wait patiently for Christmas Eve, when the *Petit* Jesus shall be placed in the manger. Deep within our hearts, we treasure the witness of our humble crèche: Christ was born of Mary, in Bethlehem, and she laid him in a manger. When the moment arrives to place the Christ Child in his tiny bed made of straw and hay stored in our barn, we welcome him with the carol:

> *Away in a manger, no crib for a bed,*
> *The little Lord Jesus laid down his sweet head.*

Throughout the Christmas season, the little Lord Jesus is present in our midst in this humble crèche, assuring each of us of his tender love for us. As we gaze at the scene and look at him with his arms outstretched, he seems to be telling us, "See how much I love you." In the crèche, he daily awaits our visit. As we draw close to him, we hear his welcome greeting: "Peace be with you."

Icon of the Nativity

The icon of the Nativity on the cover of this book, inspired by the Greek/Russian iconographic tradition, was created for our monastery chapel by a well-known iconographer and friend, Olga Poloukhine. It is the icon that is placed for veneration on the iconstand all throughout the Christmas season. In the icon, Olga relates the account of Christ's birth as told in the sacred Scriptures. The icon portrays all creation, in one way or another, forever changed by this transcendental event, henceforth called to participate in the mystery of Christ's birth. The angels give thanks with their chant, the heavens provide a star, the Wise Men give their gifts of gold, frankincense, and myrrh. The humble shepherds give their praise, wonder, and amazement, the earth gives the cave, and humanity gives a Virgin Mother.

The Nativity icon is one that contains many scenes. First, it emphasizes the role of the *Theotokos*, the Mother of Jesus. She is placed in the center and is the largest figure in the icon. There, she is resting quietly next to Baby Jesus. The three stars, proclaiming her virginity before, during, and after the Nativity, are on her garments. The Baby Jesus, right in the center of the icon, is in swaddling clothes and is lying in a manger. In the background is the dark cave where he was born, a symbol of the cave where later he would be for three days in the tomb. In the cave are an ox and a donkey guarding the newborn infant. Even though the Gospels say nothing of the cave, this knowledge comes to us from an ancient Church tradition. Neither do the Gospels speak of the ox and the donkey, but all icons and crèches of the Nativity include these animals. Including the animals in the icon fulfills the prophecy of Isaiah 1:3, "An ox knows his owner, and an ass, its master's manger; but Israel does not know, my people has not understood." The long ray of light from the star points directly to the cave. This ray comes from the star and travels to all parts of the world. It teaches that this bright star is an astronomical happening and is a messenger from heaven announcing the birth of Jesus.

On the left side of the icon is another scene. The Wise Men, who were led by the star, arrive to the scene riding horses to bring their gifts of gold, frankincense, and myrrh to Jesus. The Wise Men seem to be of different ages. These details teach us that regardless of age, appearance, or culture, the Savior brings the good news to everyone.

Opposite the Wise Men is the scene with the humble shepherds. An angel proclaims the glad tidings to them. Across from the shepherd's scene is the heavenly choir of angels. They are giving glory to God in song. The angels serve two purposes in the Nativity of Christ: they glorify God and they also announce the good news to the entire world.

The background shows a very rugged terrain. This tries to represent the Judean desert land of that area. Joseph could not find room in Bethlehem, so they went outside of Bethlehem to a cave. The deserted rocky mountain formation serves as a background for the event that is to take place.

In the lower part of the icon are two more scenes. In the right-hand corner are the two women Joseph brought to take care of the Christ Child. They are bathing the child just as any baby is bathed after birth. The human aspect of Jesus' Nativity is certainly shown in this detail.

Opposite the bathing-of-Jesus scene sits a sad and worried Joseph. He is not part of the central group of the Christ Child and the *Theotokos*. Joseph is not the natural father, only the foster one. Joseph seems troubled and despondent. There is an old man talking to him. The old man is Satan. Satan can appear disguised under many forms. Here he is represented as an old man who is tempting and disturbing the humble, righteous Joseph. Satan is telling him that a virgin birth is impossible and a lie, that he's a fool to believe in a fantasy. This story, as we know, also comes from an ancient tradition. The sad Joseph shows us not only his personal predicament, but also the dilemma all humans face in accepting that which is beyond human reason.

The tree, which is in the middle of the lower part of the icon, is a symbol of the tree of Jesse. This tree refers to Isaiah 11:1–2, "But a shoot shall sprout from the stump of Jesse, and from his roots a bud shall blossom. The spirit of the LORD shall rest upon him." King David was often mentioned as the son of Jesse and Jesus was from the house of David.

The icon of the Nativity reminds us to praise, glorify, and offer thanksgiving to God the Father for the birth of the Savior we contemplate in the icon. Each year, the celebration of Christmas serves to remind us that Christ was born to save all of us.

> *Today a Virgin gives birth*
> *to him who is above all being,*
> *and the earth offers a cave to him*
> *whom the world cannot contain.*
> *Angels with shepherds give glory*
> *and Magi journey led by a star.*
> *For unto us is born a young child,*
> *the pre-eternal God!*
>
> KONTAKION OF THE NATIVITY

The Christmas Tree

The world is like a Christmas tree,
Each one of us, a light.
To what degree we love God's Son
We are dim or bright.
We have no power of our own.
We can never shine
Until he fills us with his love,
His Christmas love, divine.

MARGARET PETERSON

Never worry about the size of your Christmas tree.
In the eyes of children, they are all thirty feet tall.

LARRY WILDE

For many people, Christmas is a state of mind. Throughout the years I have met people who talk of Christmas in July and people who all year long seem to be on the lookout for special ornaments to decorate their trees when Christmas arrives. Decorating the tree each year is something that both young and old look forward to doing. For many this is the touchstone of the season's celebration. Putting up the tree often brings back many cherished memories of family gatherings, of traditions and festivities from the past. Each of us loves to hold on to those cherished memories. They seem to provide lovely feelings about the season that linger on and on every time we encounter a Christmas tree.

Legend has it that the practice of honoring and decorating trees goes back to early pagan times, long before the arrival of Christianity. The people of northern European countries had the custom of decorating their trees during the winter months. This custom provided a special meaning to them during the long months of harsh weather. In ancient times, the people not only decorated their pine or spruce trees, they went further and used evergreen branches to decorate their doors, windows, chimneys, or other entrances. In the pagan tradition of many of these people, it was believed that evergreen kept away demons and witches, ghosts and evil spirits. Evergreens were also symbols of the sun god. Eventually, spring and summer would return, the time of the year when the sun god is strong and when greenery is found all around. The pagans also decorated their trees to celebrate the winter solstice, especially on the feast of Saturnalia, the god that protected farmers and

their crops. The celebration reminded them that soon again their farms, fields, and orchards should turn green and fruitful. Decorating their trees and homes with beautiful evergreen boughs was used to mark the occasion.

The Christian custom of decorating a tree at Christmastime seems to have started sometime around 1521, in Alsace, which at that time was part of Germany. For these German Christians, the decorated tree became the living symbol of the fusion of two opposite traditions: the pagan and the Christian one. The Christmas tree also became the symbol of the tree of paradise, itself a symbol of the life-giving tree of the cross. These German Christians, both Protestant and Catholic, brought the tree inside their homes on Christmas Eve. The tree was then decorated with apples and other fruits, with lighted candles and glass balls. During the holy night, families kept joyful vigil around the tree and the crèche, and upon returning from midnight Mass, they all again sat around the tree partaking of sweets, cakes, and other delicacies prepared especially for the occasion. A star was placed on the top of the tree, a symbol of Christ, the Light of the World, who shone bright on that night many centuries ago in the tiny village of Bethlehem. From Alsace, the custom spread to the rest of Germany and other countries, and in the eighteenth century it was brought to America by the first German immigrants. It is said that the Pennsylvania German settlers mounted community trees in their midst as early as 1747. From these early German settlers, the custom spread to the rest of the country, and in the twentieth century decorating a Christmas tree became an all-American tradition. The arrival of electricity brought about the custom of using small lights to decorate and give a certain glow to the trees. Today, when the Christmas season arrives, beautifully decorated trees are found in many homes, town squares, and villages across the country.

Christmas trees are very special in the monastery, where one is placed and decorated in the chapel, and a second one is arranged in the parlor where our guests are received. One of the more enjoyable activities at this time of the year is decorating the monastery Christmas trees. During these days, many people go to extremes with certain decorations, but in the monastery we adhere to a certain monastic sobriety. Therefore, we keep the decorations simple and in accordance with basic good taste. The Christmas tree and the crèche are placed close together, reminding us that both are there to speak to us of the birth of Christ. On the evening of December 24, when the cold of winter is deeply felt and the sun is about to set, the

Christmas tree is lighted and blessed in the monastery. The bells begin to ring joyfully, announcing to the locality the good tidings of Christ's birth. As we process into the chapel to sing the solemn vespers of the Nativity, we encounter the tree shining and glowing in a myriad of little lights. This adds a particular festive touch to our Christmas celebration. Later in the evening, after midnight Mass, we sit around the Christmas tree in the community room, share a cup of hot cocoa and Christmas cookies, rejoicing all along that Christ is born and that he is indeed in our midst. Christ is born; glorify him!

The monastery Christmas tree is not just a seasonal decoration; it is rather a powerful witness to the fact that Christ is the true tree of life. Just as Adam and Eve fell in disgrace by eating the fruit of the forbidden tree, today humanity is reborn to a new life by the power of another tree, the tree of the cross. Christ, the author of the new creation, is planted deep in the womb of a Virgin Mother and from there he emerges at Christmas, inviting one and all to partake of the fruits of the tree of life.

O Christmas tree, O Christmas tree!
Thou tree most fair and lovely!
The sight of thee at Christmastide
Spreads hope and gladness far and wide.
O Christmas tree, O Christmas tree!
Thou tree most fair and lovely.
O Christmas tree, O Christmas tree!
Thou hast a wondrous message:
Thou dost proclaim the Savior's birth,
Good will to men and peace on earth.
O Christmas tree, O Christmas tree!
Thou hast a wondrous message.

O TANNENBAUM, A GERMAN CHRISTMAS FOLK SONG

Christmas Music: The Carols

There's a song in the air!
There's a star in the sky!
There's a mother's deep prayer
And a baby's low cry!
And the star rains its fire while the beautiful sing,
For the manger of Bethlehem cradles a king.
There's a tumult of joy
O'er the wonderful birth,
For the Virgin's sweet boy
Is the Lord of the earth,
Ay! the star runs its fire while the beautiful sing,
In the homes of the nations that Jesus is King!

JOSIAH G. HOLLAND

Let all the world
In eve'ry corner sing:
Today the Lord is born,
My God and my King!

ANONYMOUS

Today Bethlehem receives him who from all times
sits next to the Father.
Today angels glorify with holy hymns the Babe that
is born, singing:
Glory to God in the highest, on earth peace, good
will among men.

CHRISTMAS BYZANTINE MATINS

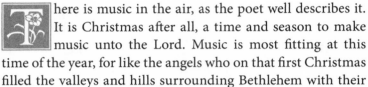 here is music in the air, as the poet well describes it. It is Christmas after all, a time and season to make music unto the Lord. Music is most fitting at this time of the year, for like the angels who on that first Christmas filled the valleys and hills surrounding Bethlehem with their chant, "Glory to God in the highest," to this day the people of the world continue to celebrate with music and song the glorious commemoration of the Lord's birth. Christians in the past, following the tradition of the synagogue and that of early days of the Church, celebrated each particular liturgical event with appropriate readings and songs of praise. So it seems natural that we also honor that almost timeless tradition and thus observe the yearly festival of the Nativity with hymns and canticles, with popular carols, and all sorts of instrumental music. Christmas music, that is, religious Christmas music, is always an invitation to deeper prayer and praise.

The deep joy we find in our Christmas music, whether it be the monastic liturgical chants, the oratorios or cantatas, or simple popular Christmas carols, is truly inspirational and deeply spiritual. It feeds our innermost soul. The music of Christmas, in my view, also fosters good fellowship and community spirit among those who worship and make music together in praise of the Lord's Nativity. Singing during Christmas is an endearing custom inherited from our forbearers, and to this day it continues to nourish our souls. What would Christmas be without the joy of its own music, those marvelous sounds of the season? Every year, when Christmas arrives, both young and old rediscover the unique joy contained in this timeless music. We look with anticipation to the joyous sounds of "Silent Night," "*Adeste Fideles*," "Angels We Have Heard on High," "Away in a Manger," and others, especially when sung at Mass, or around the tree or the family table. Singing our lovely Christmas music, particularly the

carols, is as much part of the season's tradition as is the crèche, the Christmas tree, reading greeting cards, or filling stockings hung by the chimney at home. All these customs, especially the music and words contained in the carols, serve to remind us of one thing: the glorious event of Christ's Incarnation, of his birth in our midst.

The music of Christmas knows no limits or restrictions when it comes to expressing or professing a profound faith in the mystery it celebrates. Furthermore, in time we discover there is a universal character to this music for believers of all generations, from all countries, climates, and continents have freely contributed compositions in their language and with their own cultural sounds to show praise and thanksgiving to God for the gift of his divine Son. It is a unique joy of the season to sing many of these carols from faraway places and to identify with our fellow Christians of other cultures. I find it inspiring when we try to sing these carols in their own rich native languages. They are genial as well as simple, and in them we discover a true spiritual treasure.

Although we are well-acquainted with the Christmas carols we hear and sing often in church, school, or family gatherings, we are not always totally familiar with their origins or the composers who wrote them. Christmastime gives us the occasion, if we so desire, to enrich our knowledge and faith by learning more about each carol, its country of origin, and of course, about the poets and composers who inspire us to sing like the angels about good tidings of peace on earth and good will to all, thus glorifying God in all things. Christmastide, I once heard, is the most "caroling" period of the entire year. In spite of the anticipated use of carols in commercial places well before Christmas itself arrives, we can't deny the fact that the songs and sounds of Christmas touch the hearts and cheer the souls not only of Christians, but of people everywhere. In the midst of an almost palpable pagan culture and totally secularized world, the humble tunes from the carols make sure the joy of the season, the hope that Christ brings to the world, and the praise of God continue to be heard.

Shout with joy to the LORD, all the earth;
break into song; sing praise.
Sing praise to the LORD with the lyre,
with the lyre and melodious song.
With trumpets and the sound of the horn
shout with joy to the King, the LORD…
Let the rivers clap their hands,
the mountains shout with them for joy,
Before the LORD who comes,
who comes to govern the earth.

PSALM 98

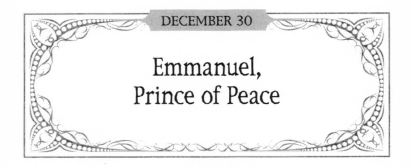

DECEMBER 30

Emmanuel,
Prince of Peace

For a child is born to us, a son is given to us;
upon his shoulder dominion rests.
They name him Wonder-Counselor, God-Hero,
Father-Forever, Prince of Peace.

ISAIAH 9:5

And suddenly there was a multitude of the heavenly
host with the angel, praising God and saying: "Glory
to God in the highest and on earth peace to those
on whom his favor rests."

LUKE 2:13–14

Today true peace came down from heaven.
Today the heavens drip honey upon the whole earth.
Today a new day dawns, the day of our redemption,
Prepared by God from ages past, the beginning
of our deliverance and of our never-ending gladness.

CHRISTMAS RESPONSORY, MATINS

t is an astonishing fact, and yet most Christians never completely acknowledge it: From the very beginning, from the prophets on, the person of the Messiah was always announced as a messenger of peace. Isaiah, in speaking of the coming Messiah, proclaims a new era of great peace and goes as far as to call him a prince of peace. On the day of the Lord's Nativity we hear once again the same message in the angels' singing: "Glory to God in the highest and on earth peace to those on whom his favor rests." Peace, not conflict, violence, or wars, the true peace that descends from heaven, is the trademark of the Messiah, the Son of God who comes to dwell among us, the prince of peace. And yet today, just as in the time of Christ, we are surrounded by noisy, cruel wars approved by our savvy politicians, by

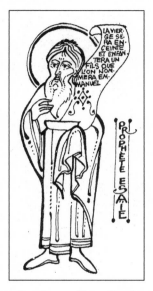

the violence that we bring upon one another, by endless deaths caused by our own troops in the name of those who represent us. Could all this be in accord with the message of the prince of peace? Could it be that he approves of this ghastly inhuman behavior we cast upon one another? These are some of the questions that an honest disciple of Christ is compelled to ask at this time when we celebrate and pay lip service to the birth of the prince of peace.

There is no doubt in my mind that Christ was opposed to every form of human violence. He plainly rebuked his disciples when they tried to defend him by saying to them, "all who take the sword will perish by the sword." The Lord, good master that he was, never minced words, and the apostles and early disciples of the Lord understood this correctly. It is told of Saint Martin of Tours, a soldier in the Roman army, that once he was baptized a Christian he lay down his sword. When he was asked why, he simply responded that now as a soldier of Christ he could no longer bear arms or kill anyone. To these early Christians the Lord's teachings were plain, clear and simple. There was no room for doubt or for reinterpreting the Lord's teachings. They knew that in the books of the Gospel the recourse to violence is never acceptable, never justified. And they have heard Isaiah's prophetic words:

> *They shall beat their swords into plowshares*
> *and their spears into pruning hooks;*
> *One nation shall not raise the sword against another,*
> *nor shall they train for war again.*
>
> ISAIAH 2:4

Our Christmas celebration is one of great hope, for we are given a clear occasion to hear again Christ's message of peace, we are given the chance to honor the prince of peace and to renew our commitment to his teachings. When Pope Paul VI came to the United Nations in New York City, he pleaded with the people of all nations to stop all wars and recourses to war. He cried out *"Jamais plus la guerre!* (War, never again. Never!)" He was not sending a personal message, he was pleading for the message of the Gospel to be heard. He was not saying this in his own name, but in the name of Christ whom he represented. He was asking all people to choose the ways of nonviolence and to walk along the path of peace traced by Christ, our master. By choosing to oppose all violence and instead live in harmony and peace with others, even our so-called enemies, we make a direct choice to foster and extend the kingdom of God, the only true kingdom. Saint Paul, in his Letter to the Romans, is explicit about this: "The kingdom of God is not a matter of food and drink, but of righteousness, peace, and joy in the holy Spirit; whoever serves Christ in this way is pleasing to God and approved by others. Let us then pursue what leads to peace and to building up one another" (Romans 14:17–19).

Our Christmas hope is a clear invitation from the Lord to become instruments of his peace, true peacemakers. In the Sermon on the Mount, hear the Lord proclaim: "Blessed are the peacemakers, for they will be called children of God." This is not pure coincidence but simply the same message conveyed by the angels on that first Christmas night. To become in truth a Christian peacemaker, after the example of the Lord himself, we must accept the risk of being controversial, countercultural, and being taken as a fool by others, just like many of Jesus' disciples before us: Saint Martin of Tours, Saint Benedict, the Desert Fathers and Mothers, Saint Francis of Assisi, and in our days, servants of God Dorothy Day, Thomas Merton, etc. All of these people were often rejected because of their evangelical views and example. It was the price they paid for true discipleship. It takes a profound faith in God's words and promises, a fierce inner fortitude, and plenty of God's grace to accept the challenge to become a peacemaker like Christ, our best model and master. Indeed, to work for peace entails accepting the ministry of reconciliation among all people, among those hostile to each other, among nations at war, among family, neighbors, and churches still in discord with each other. There is nothing romantic about becoming a true peacemaker. It implies hard work, dying to self daily, fidelity to prayer, extreme humility, and total obedience to God's word. Only by doing this can we become, in the words of Saint Francis of Assisi, "instruments of his peace."

Our challenge, as Christians, is to renew our commitment to the Christmas message sung by the angels and to do everything possible to foster and implement peace and harmony among all the people of the earth, for he who comes as Savior of all is also the prince of peace to all.

A Hymn to the Prince of Peace

Behold a broken world, we pray,
Where want and war increase,
And grant, Lord, in this our day,
The ancient dream of peace:
A dream of swords to sickles bent,
Of spears to scythe and spade,
The weapons of our warfare spent,
A world of peace remade.
Where every battle flag is furled
And every trumpet stilled,
Where wars shall cease in all the world.
A waking dream fulfilled.
No force of arms shall there prevail
Nor justice cease her sway;
Nor shall their loftiest visions fail
The dreamers of the day.
O Prince of Peace, who died to save,
A lost world to redeem,
And rose in triumph from the grave,
Behold our waking dream.
Bring, Lord, your better world to birth,
Your kingdom, love's domain;
Where peace with God, and peace on earth,
And peace eternal reign.

A Christmas Prayer

BY THE TWELFTH-CENTURY
CISTERCIAN MONK GUERRIC D'IGNY
(TRANSLATED FROM THE FRENCH)

The twelfth-century Cistercian monks were known for their strong attachment to the mystery of the Incarnation. This is particularly noticeable in their writings and sermons concerning Advent, Christmas, Epiphany, etc. One of these extraordinary Cistercian figures from the Middle Ages was Blessed Guerric d'Igny, who composed five sermons to honor the mystery of the Nativity of Christ. In his beautiful and poetic sermons, Blessed Guerric emphasizes God's pure and gratuitous gift in the Incarnation of his only begotten Son. For Guerric, the mystery of the Incarnation is the supreme testament of God's boundless generosity, of his infinite love. The Lord of heaven and earth had nothing to gain personally from the fact of becoming human, incarnate, yet he does it in order to share our lives, our human condition, and to give himself entirely to us.

Christmas celebrates this gift of God's love, of his need to give himself to us and become like us. When we behold the Infant Savior in the crèche, we behold the truth that God is love, and that in his love for humankind he accepted becoming a little child just like the rest of us. It is to this tiny Infant of the crèche that Blessed Guerric, at the end of one of his several Christmas sermons, addresses the following prayer:

O most sweet and good Child Jesus,

What treasures of loving kindness You have stored up for those who fear You, those who trust in You, when You have already shown so much care for those who don't even know You. It is indeed, incomparable sweetness, ineffable tenderness to look upon God as a Child created for love, a God of majesty and glory become like me not only in a human form, but even in the helplessness of childhood.

Truly Child God, my Guardian and my God, You are all sweetness and the object of my desire. Nevertheless the tenderness of your small body makes You sweeter still to me. This tenderness makes you accessible to children who are not yet able to take solid food. It is sweet and delightful for us to reflect on You, O God Child, who came to heal and sweeten the rancor, bitterness, or enmity that might exist among us. For I am sure that where there is understanding and recollection of this divine sweetness, there is no room for anger or sadness. All bitterness and hostility due to our faults is swept away as we contemplate your Presence. And so, as children newly born, too, let us praise our newborn Lord. With heart and voice in accord let the lips of children and babes be vocal with praise to the Infant Lord Jesus Christ. To him with the Father and the Holy Spirit may there be praise and jubilation forever and unto ages of ages. Amen.

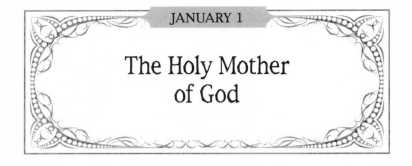

The Holy Mother of God

O marvelous exchange! Man's Creator has become man, born of a Virgin. We have been made sharers in the divinity of Christ who humbled himself to share our humanity.

ANTIPHON II VESPERS OF THE FEAST

Your blessed and fruitful virginity is like the bush, flaming and unburned, which Moses saw on Sinai, pray for us, holy Mother of God!

ANTIPHON II VESPERS OF THE FEAST

There is a rare, special calmness that seems rather appropriate for this time of the year. It is the calmness that emanates from our winter quietude. Outdoors, in nature, all is silent, all is calm, dormant, peaceful. Blessed are they who can truly appreciate the graces of winter's quiet, its solitude, its silence, its peace.

Today is the first day of a new year, and it is also the feast of the *Theotokos*, our Lady, the holy Mother of God. Whatever the new year has in store for us, it's a good omen that we begin its counting under our Lady's unfailing protection. She reminds us daily that all time is God's time; we must not cling to it as we do to possessions. On the contrary, we must learn to use time wisely during our earthly pilgrimage, following Christ's and our Lady's own examples. As we enter into the new year, it is good to consider seriously the wise use of whatever length of time is allotted to us, how we spend our days and try to discern what our ultimate goals are. New Year's Day should not be just an occasion for partying and celebration. To make it memorable, worthwhile, it should include a time for serious reflection on life's ultimate purpose, a time to ponder how we can enhance our future days and make them richer with the grace and gifts bestowed on us by the Lord.

It is so fitting that today, on the octave of Christmas, we honor in a special way the memory of God's holy Mother, the *Theotokos*. The immense mystery of the Incarnation would have been impossible without her. Jesus' father is God himself, but he needed a human mother to become man to be born among us. Mary, the humble maiden from Nazareth, was assigned that role; she accepted it willingly, in complete submission and cooperation with God's plan. Therefore, from that moment on, all generations call her blessed.

We find great consolation in the presence of the Mother of God in our lives. It is very real. She is our mother, our friend, our helper, our living example of true Gospel living, our refuge in time of danger, a solace in time of affliction. She is also a luminous guide when we find ourselves submerged under the shadows of darkness and despair. On our pilgrimage toward God's kingdom, her maternal presence dispels our doubts, our loneliness. She provides the strength and encouragement needed for the remainder of the journey. We walk, but never alone, for the most holy *Theotokos* walks along the path of life with us. If we learn to keep quiet and remain silent, if we don't interfere or make much fuss about ourselves, we should be able to feel again and again her consoling presence as we pray to Christ, our God, and offer him the gift of his holy Mother:

> *What shall we offer You, O Christ,*
> *Who for our sake has appeared on earth as a man?*
> *Every creature made by You, offers You thanks.*
> *The angels offer You a song,*
> *The heavens, a star,*
> *The Wise Men, their gifts.*
> *The shepherds, their wonder.*
> *The earth, a cave.*
> *The wilderness, a manger.*
> *And we, what could we offer You?*
> *We offer You a Virgin Mother!*
> *O eternal God, have mercy on us!*

JANUARY 2

A Christmas Season Meditation

BY SAINT AELRED DE RIEVAULX
(TRANSLATED FROM THE FRENCH)

Fear not, O people of God!
Do not tremble as you face the devil's tyranny,
or the corruption of original sin.
Instead, receive the Lord your God,
As the wondrous sign
Of the conception by a virgin:
"Behold, he says, a virgin shall conceive
and give birth to a child."
He (or she) who believes in this conception by a virgin,
Will also easily believe that she
Could not have given birth
To other but the Son of God.
This is why Isaiah adds in his prophecy
"And he shall be called Emmanuel,"
which means, "God is with us."
Yes, certainly, God is with us!
Till now, God was above us,
God was against us,
But today, he is Emmanuel!

Today God is with us in our own human nature,
With us by his grace,
With us in our infirmities,
With us in his sweetness,
With us in our misery,
With us in his mercy,
With us in his charity,
With us in his tenderness,
With us in his affection for us,
With us in his compassion.
O Emmanuel, O God with us!
Have pity on Adam's children,
Be with us always,
O God with us!

Saint Aelred, like Blessed Guerric d'Igny, was a Cistercian monk from the Middle Ages. In 1134, he entered the abbey of Rievaulx, which was founded by the monks from Clairvaux. He became its abbot in 1147. He was greatly influenced by Saint Bernard, one of the stars of the Cistercian sky, and wrote a well-known treatise on the art of spiritual friendship. He died in 1167.

The Monastery Sheepfold and the Legend of the Lamb

Sleep, Thou little Child of Mary,
Some fair day
Wilt Thou, as Thou wert a brother,
Come away
Over hills and over hollow?
All the lambs will up and follow,
Follow but for love of Thee,
Lov'st Thou me?

SONG OF A LITTLE SHEPHERD AT BETHLEHEM,
BY JOSEPHINE PEABODY

very year, as we read the Christmas story, we are interiorly led to the contemplation of the mystery that transpires in a humble cave, in a tiny manger, in the little town of Bethlehem. The biblical writer relates the event of angels singing and proclaiming peace on earth, of shepherds and their flock of sheep hurrying to the cave to witness the event and adore a little child. And as we read the story, we, too, are awestruck by the wonderful proceedings taking place right before our eyes.

As we witness the event, great lessons seem to spring forth

from the small, humble people and elements we encounter in Bethlehem: a small town, a cave, a bright star, a humble maiden, a carpenter father, simple country shepherds and their flock, angels singing above in the skies, etc. All of them, both nature and people, are most privileged at being the first ones to gaze upon the human face of God. Humble beasts, like the oxen and donkey, like the shepherds' sheep, are the first ones chosen to pay homage to the Lord of all creation. What lessons are there for us, about God's own humility and about his utter preference for the humble, poor, and lowly!

The story of the Bethlehem shepherds and sheep is one easily comprehensible to us in this monastery. Like the shepherds,

we also keep and tend to a small flock of sheep. Christmastime, therefore, is very special to us and to each sheep in our sheepfold. I often compare our barn where the sheep find shelter during our long, rough winters to the humble cave or stable of Bethlehem. Indeed, when at Christmas we place a small statue of the Baby Jesus in a dark corner of the barn so the sheep have their own crèche, the entire barn becomes a small Bethlehem! Throughout Christmastide, our sheep pay homage to their Lord and Creator, and one of the things we do ourselves each year is to read to our friends and those who visit us in front of the barn crèche, with all the sheep in attendance:

It was Christmas night, and the little lamb had nothing to offer the tiny Christ Child who shared his stable. Suddenly, the lamb noticed the baby's blankets were thin and poor, and the straw upon which he lay offered little warmth and comfort. So the lamb very quietly snuggled close to the Baby Jesus and sheltered him from the cold. The Christ Child smiled and touched the lamb's shaggy coat, whereupon it became transformed into soft, curly wool. From that day to this, all sheep wear the warm symbol of Christ's gratitude for the selfless action of the one small lamb on that first Christmas night.

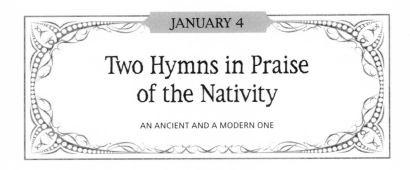

Two Hymns in Praise of the Nativity

AN ANCIENT AND A MODERN ONE

Holy Infant, Light From the East

BY SAINT EPHREM THE SYRIAN

His light shone out over the east;
Persia was enlightened by the star:
His Epiphany gave good tidings and invited her,
"He is come for the sacrifice that brings joy to all."

The star of light hastened and came and dawned
through the darkness, and summoned them
that all the people should come and exult
in the great Light that has come down to earth.

One envoy from among the stars
the firmament sent to proclaim to them,
to the sons of Persia, that they might make ready
to meet the King and to worship him.

Great Assyria when she perceived it
called to the Magi and said to them,
"Take gifts and go, honor him
the great King who in Judea is dawned."

The princes of Persia, exulting,
carried gifts from their region;
and they brought to the Son of the Virgin
gold and myrrh and frankincense.

They entered and found him as a child
as he dwelt in the house of the lowly woman;
and they drew near and worshipped with gladness,
and brought near before him their treasures...

Let the Church sing with rejoicing,
"Glory in the Birth of the Highest,
by whom the world above and the world below are
*   illumined!"*
Blessed be he in whose birth made all glad!

Cradle Hymn

BY ISAAC WATTS

Hush, my dear, lie still and slumber;
Holy angels guard thy bed;
Heavenly blessings without number
Gently falling on thy head.

Sleep, my babe, thy food and raiment,
House and home, thy friends provide;
All without thy care, or payment,
All thy wants are well-supplied.

How much better thou'rt attended
Than the Son of God could be,
When from heaven he descended,
And became a child like thee!

Soft and easy is thy cradle;
Coarse and hard thy Savior lay,
When his birthplace was a stable,
And his softest bed was hay.

See the kindly shepherds 'round him,
Telling wonders from the sky!
When they sought him, there they found him,
With his Virgin Mother by.
See the lovely babe a-dressing;
Lovely infant, how he smiled!
When he wept, the mother's blessing
Soothed and hushed the holy child.

Lo, he slumbers in his manger,
Where the honest oxen fed;
—Peace, my darling! Here's no danger!
Here's no ox a-near thy bed!

Mayst thou live to know and fear him,
Trust and love him all thy days;
Then go dwell forever near him,
See his face, and sing his praise!

I could give thee thousand kisses,
Hoping what I most desire;
Not a mother's fondest wishes
Can to greater joys aspire.

Rejoice

(A POEM FOR THE EVE OF THE EPIPHANY)

Glory to God in the highest
And peace on earth among men.
For a child is born in a manger
In the town of Bethlehem.
This darling baby boy,
And everyone was welcomed
To share in Mary's joy.
The journey was far for many who came
But this baby was special by far.
They were given no maps or direction
Only to follow the star.
And there little Jesus so peacefully lay
All gazing with wonder and awe.
Truly this was the Messiah
And they marveled at what they saw.

HELEN PARKER

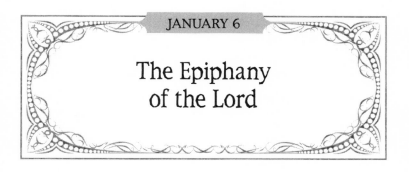

The Epiphany of the Lord

Arise! Shine, for your light has come,
the glory of the LORD has dawned upon you.
Though darkness covers the earth,
and thick clouds, the peoples,
Upon you the LORD will dawn,
and over you his glory will be seen.
Nations shall walk by your light,
kings by the radiance of your dawning.

ISAIAH 60:1–3

Earth spreads out its wide spaces
To welcome its Creator,
He receives glory from the angels on high
And from the heavens a star points to him.
The Magi arrive to the cave with gifts,
And the Lord is manifested to the whole world.

BYZANTINE COMPLINE

ur winter air is perfectly still. I enjoy this seasonal stillness and drink deeply from its healthy pure air. It is truly a gift from above, and I just hope it remains with us for a long time. In the great outdoors, well beyond the confines of the monastic land, Mother Nature is simply silent, quiet, all white and very clean. It is picture perfect! In all honesty, what I appreciate the most at this time of the year is its gift of quiet stillness. That is precious, and there is not enough money in the world to pay for its real value!

Today is the feast of the Epiphany, the twelfth day after Christmas. The splendor of this feast recalls God's manifestation to all people, to the whole world. On Christmas Day, God's goodness became visible to us under the form of a baby, in the sacred humanity of Christ, God's only begotten Son and the Father's true image and substance. Through faith, we know the mystery of the Incarnation, and Christ's appearance in our midst changed forever the course of human history. God appeared in our world as a small baby, but he came to it as Savior. He came to save us!

In the Latin-Mediterranean countries, the feast of the Epiphany is commonly known as the Feast of the Three Kings, after the Gospel story of the Magi who journeyed to Bethlehem. Guided by a bright, unusual star, they came from afar to the humble cave of Bethlehem to render homage to a tiny child, the king of kings. In the Gospel story, the evangelists make sure to imply that the Magi represented the gentiles, thus Jesus did not just come to save Israel's Chosen People, but to save all humankind, Jews and gentiles alike. The gifts the Magi offered to the tiny infant are pregnant with meaning, with very special implications, and thus the liturgy reminds us repeatedly of the value of these symbols. The gift of gold symbolizes that from now on Christ alone is the Lord and king of the new Israel. The gift of frankincense symbolizes the divinity of Christ: He is both true man and true God. Incense, in the ancient religious tradition, was only offered to God, and thus now to Jesus, the Christ. The gift of myrrh represents the sacred ointments that one day shall be used at Christ's burial, for Jesus, the Lord's Anointed, is also the sacrificial Lamb of God, the one by whose death the world shall be cleansed of its sins. A text from the Byzantine Compline of the season poignantly points to these symbols:

> *The Three Kings, the first among the gentiles*
> *   to receive your revelation,*
> *Present you with gifts at your birth in Bethlehem,*
> *You who were born from a mother that knew no*
> *   wedlock.*
> *With myrrh they announced your death.*
> *With gold they symbolize your royal power,*
> *And with frankincense they proclaim your divinity!*

There are many monastic customs associated with the feast of the Epiphany that sometimes vary from monastery to monastery, depending on their location or country of origin. One very ancient custom that remains alive to this day in most monasteries is the solemn announcement during the liturgy of the dates for the movable feasts of the coming year: Ash Wednesday, Easter, Ascension, Pentecost, and, at the end, the first Sunday of Advent. The announcement proclaims, "As we have recently rejoiced over the birth of our Lord Jesus Christ, now through the mercy of God, we can look forward to the happiness that will stem from the resurrection of the same Lord and Savior."

There are also other customs with a more mundane aspect to them, such as the reception of gifts by the children, making them believe the Three Kings have passed by their home and rewarded their good behavior with timely gifts.

In France, one lovely Epiphany custom that survives to this day is the presentation of the *gateau des rois* (cake of the Three Kings) at the family table. Usually, a piece of cake is set aside for Jesus, and this piece is given to the first poor hungry per-

son who knocks at the door asking for food. A touching aspect of this charming custom is the search for a small fava bean or medal carefully hidden in the cake. The person who bakes the cake hides the small bean somewhere inside the cake, and whoever finds the bean is declared "king" or "queen" for a day. Those present at the table, the whole family, then toast the honoree with a sweet dessert wine and the king or queen moves forward to preside at the head of the table. In France, endless recipes exist for this *gateau des rois*, since it is a very popular and much-appreciated old custom, one that brings joy to the hearts of all the participants, young and old, one that reminds everyone of God's loving appearance among his people.

O Father, may that Holy star
Grow every year more bright,
And send its glorious beams afar
To fill the world with light.

WILLIAM CULLEN BRYANT

Christmas Reflections
for All Year

Glory to you, O Lord,
Who have come into the world
To save all humankind.

SAINT JOHN DAMASCENE,
EIGHTH CENTURY

It wasn't too long ago that we decided to undertake a spiritual journey that makes us walk the Advent steps to Christmas, to Epiphany, and last but not least to the Theophany summit. It seems it all started only yesterday, and here we are now, past Epiphany and on the very threshold of the Theophany that shall bring the Christmas season to its official conclusion. There is a bit of nostalgia, a sense of letting it go that we all feel as we approach the final days of this spiritually rich pilgrimage. And though the liturgy is ready to tell us to move on to ordinary time and start preparing for Lent and Easter, there is no reason why we couldn't make the effort to carry something of the Christmas spirit all year. The Christmas spirit is unique, special, uplifting, inspiring, and always very comforting. We must strive somehow to let it pervade our lives, in one form or another, every day of the year.

Christmas is a celebration of the mystery of the Incarnation, of the birth of Christ in our world, and somehow Christ must continue to be born daily in our lives, in the innermost of our hearts. The special grace that Christmas bestows on us is precisely this unique instinct of the heart. There is nothing comparable to Christmas to provide us that unique realization of its true meaning—the magic stirring of the heart that deepens itself to embrace the very core of life. It is only in the very depths of our hearts that we can grasp and absorb the transcendental significance of that first Christmas.

It is with the heart's ear, as Saint Benedict points out, that we can continue to savor the peaceful music and message from the angels' choir on that first Christmas night. And it is with the heart's eyes that we must glance at the ray of light in a wintry star-struck sky and depict the secret path the light traces, a path that, if we all follow, can change the entire world.

In the secret sanctuary of our hearts, we learn from the Holy Spirit that to carry out the Christmas spirit all year we must daily put into practice the teachings from the master. We must make recourse to the open book of the Gospels and there find our guide and daily nourishment. From the Gospel, the heart learns the art of Christian living in the concrete: to be kind, humble, and gentle of heart like the master, to seek out and console those who are abandoned and forgotten, to dismiss suspicion of others and replace it with trust, to share what we have with those who have not, to never rebuke but only reply kindly, to show our loyalty to our families and communities in word and deeds, to keep our promises to God as he keeps his with us, to find daily time for prayer, reading, and reflection, to learn to forgive and forego all grudges and to love our enemies and those who do us wrong, to listen to God's word daily, to shy away from greed, envy, lies, pretension, deceit, and every form of malice, to never judge others, to trust God always and in all situations, to prefer others to ourselves, to seek not the first place but the last one as the Gospel teaches, to take up the arms of the spirit against every form of human violence, to avoid pride and self-complacency, to welcome the stranger or undocumented immigrant as one would welcome Christ, to express our gratitude to the Lord and to others daily, to worship the Lord in the quiet of our hearts and with the community of the Church, to gladden the hearts of those we come into contact with, to rejoice often in the beauty and wonder of nature, to love silence and practice patience, to speak and act with love toward all, to deepen our faith, our hope, our love for God and our neighbor daily, to live in peace with everyone, and to prefer Christ above all things. These are the attributes of a disciple of Jesus, these are the lessons we can learn from the Gospel and that we must try to exemplify in our daily lives, thus making the Christmas spirit truly present every day of the year.

The Christmas Heart

Lord, let me keep a Christmas heart,
That, 'mid the tumult of the throng,
Still hears the echo, clear and sweet,
of angels' song!
Lord, let me keep a Christmas heart,
That hears and sees another's need,
And strives each day to follow Thee
In word and deed!
Lord, let me keep a Christmas heart,
To light with joy the children's eyes,
And know the Christ Child, though he come
In humble guise!
So may I know the joy within
The wise men, coming from afar,
Knew, when at last, o'er Bethlehem
They saw thy star!
So may I keep thy birthday, Lord!
In all I say, in all I do!
A Christmas heart of faith and love
The whole year through!

GRACE BUSH

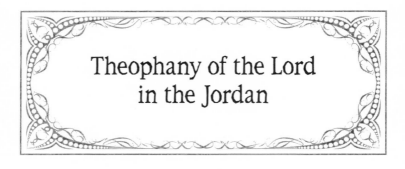

Theophany of the Lord in the Jordan

When in the Jordan You were baptized, O Lord,
The mystery of the Trinity was made manifest.
For the voice of the Father bore witness to You
And called you his beloved Son
And the Spirit, in the form of a dove,
Confirmed the truth of his words.
O Christ our God, who revealed Yourself in the Jordan,
You have enlightened the world, Glory to you.

TROPARION OF THE FEAST

n the middle of winter's gloom, and in the coldest time of the year, a brightness rises and shines in our midst. It is the feast of the Lord's Theophany, his baptism in the river Jordan, the culmination of the Christmas season. After Theophany, liturgically speaking, we shall enter the long period of ordinary time. Just a bit earlier, faith and hope were our principal guides during our wandering into the Advent desert, much love and prayer permeated our celebration of the joyful days of the Nativity, and now we finally arrive at our destination, at the summit of it all, in the glorious manifestation of the Trinity during the baptism of the Lord.

During this very special moment that Jesus accepts the baptism of John in the Jordan, the supreme mystery of all—the Trinity—is totally present, and reveals itself for the first time in the New Testament. The one true God is essentially three persons: Father, Son, and Holy Spirit. Already during Compline of the Theophany prefeast, we hear a hymn proclaim:

> *Let streams of tears wear out our eyes*
> *Let us cleanse our souls from the filth, O believer,*
> *For we shall see Christ,*
> *The light from the threefold light,*
> *Coming to the Jordan to be baptized.*
> *The Father will bear witness from heaven above,*
> *And the Holy Spirit will descend upon him*
> *In the form of a shining dove.*

As we have learned from our prior feast celebration, Epiphany and Theophany mean manifestation—God's manifestation to all people, his appearance in the world. Truly, this feast of the Lord's Theophany has a total cosmic significance. Baptism is a mystery, a symbol of a deeper reality, one that grants us sanctification and total renewal. Through his baptism in the Jordan, Christ came to sanctify the whole of creation. He came to redeem and renew wounded, sinful humanity. When Jesus plunges in the depths of the Jordan, all things are made new. His humble reception of water from the hands of John the Baptizer reveals the depths and purpose of his coming into our world.

The early Fathers express beautifully, more than anyone else, the mystical and ontological cosmic implications of the Lord's baptism. Saint Justin writes: "When Jesus came to the river

Jordan, where John was baptizing, he stepped down into the water and a fire ignited the waters of the Jordan." Saint Irenaeus implies that at that precise moment in the Jordan, the moment of his baptism, the Father anoints the whole entire cosmos. Saint Irenaeus writes that the Father bestows upon the Son the name "Christ" "because the Father anointed and adorned all things

through him." This cosmic anointing taking place today in the Jordan is already seen even earlier by the author of the Letter to the Colossians: "For in him were created all things in heaven and on earth, the visible and the invisible, whether thrones or dominions or principalities or powers; all things were created through him and for him. He is before all things, and in him all things hold together" (1:16–17). The cosmic anointing in the Jordan has a definite ontological effect on the whole cosmos: All people, all nature, all worlds and planets are touched and affected by it.

Saint Ephrem, that humble monk, mystic, and poet from Syria, uses the womb image to express the mystery at hand in the Jordan. Poetically, he writes:

The river in which Christ was baptized
conceives him again symbolically:
The moist womb of the water
Conceived him in purity,
bore him in chastity,
made him go up in glory.
In the pure womb of the river
you should recognize Mary,
the daughter of Man,
who conceived, having known no man,
who gave birth without intercourse,
who brought up, thorough a gift,
the Lord of that gift.
As the Daystar in the river,
The bright one in the tomb,
He shone forth on the mountaintop
And gave brightness too in the womb;
He dazzled as he went up from the river
And enlightened the world by his ascent.

Saint Ephrem, with a keen mystic sense, associates Christ's baptism and manifestation in the Jordan to the other events and mysteries in his life: Incarnation, transfiguration, death, resurrection, and ascension. Finally, Saint Ephrem, with that unique intuition of his, links the event of the Jordan to Pentecost, to our baptism, and the Eucharist:

Fire and Spirit are in the womb of her who bore you,
   O Christ.
Fire and Spirit are in the river in which you were
   baptized.

Fire and spirit are in our baptism,
And in the bread and cup is fire and the Holy Spirit.

On this glorious feast of the Theophany, a feast on which we discover a river ablaze with fire, a feast in which the mystery of God is revealed as a communion of the three persons, we discover the humble Christ, our manifested Lord, becoming one like us in all things. Though totally sinless, he enters the waters of the Jordan to identify with our fallen condition and to give us an example of what we, too, must do. He gently invites us to enter into the mystery of our own baptism, a baptism of water and fire, by which we are made and renewed in the image and likeness of God. The Holy Spirit confers new life upon us through the sacraments, and through them he opens wide the doors to God's kingdom.

Candlemas Eve

Adorn your bridal chamber O Sion...
Greet Mary, the Gate of heaven, with loving salutation;
For she carried the King of glory, the new Light.
In the temple stands the Virgin, embracing in her arms
*   the eternal Son*
Begotten before the day-star.
The elder Simeon welcomes him warmly into his arms
And proclaims him to the nations.

ANCIENT ANTIPHON OF THE FEAST

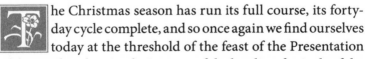

he Christmas season has run its full course, its forty-day cycle complete, and so once again we find ourselves today at the threshold of the feast of the Presentation of the Lord in the temple. It is one of the loveliest festivals of the liturgical year, one interlaced with biblical accounts, beautiful poetry, and tender lyrics. It is all about a most unusual encounter between a forty-day-old babe and his parents with two octogenarians: Simeon and Anna, who patiently waited days, months, and years for his arrival.

Here in the monastery we are busy preparing for tomorrow's celebration. It is a very important festival in the monastic calendar!

All the oil lamps in front of our many icons need to be cleaned and refilled with oil, the old candles need to be trimmed or replaced, the chapel needs to be made proper by the time we sing the first vespers of the feast. It is also the time to replace the Theophany icon with that of the Presentation. In this icon, we rediscover the familiar faces of those we fiercely love: the Child Jesus, his parents, Mary and Joseph, the elder Simeon and the prophetess Anna. This icon is like a cherished picture in the family album!

The oil lamps and the candles that burn during our daily Offices are treasured symbols of our love, piety, and attachment to the persons represented in the icons. We burn them in front of their icons, and they convey to them our love and affection. Oil lamps and candles are very expressive, very spiritual, and a must in the devotional life of a monastery. For one thing, they inspire holiness, and they also daily lift our hearts and minds to prayer. The steady flames from our lamps and candles speak to us of the intangible presence represented in the icon. The light from the lamps and candles reminds us that a mystery is present, and we leave it at that, for we are comforted by that fact. Often, it is most comforting to me to think that long after we leave our place of worship and continue with other daily duties, the oil lamps continue their watchful vigil in front of our beloved icons, silently pleading for us before God, his holy Mother, and the saints, God's own friends and our intercessors.

> *We magnify You, O Christ, Giver of Life,*
> *And we venerate your most Pure Mother,*
> *Who on this day according to the Law*
> *Brought You into the temple of the Lord.*

THE MAGNIFICATION

The Hypapante: The Presentation of the Lord in the Temple

Rejoice, O Virgin Theotokos, Full of grace!
From you shone forth the Sun of Justice, Christ our God.
Thus enlightening those who sat in darkness.
Rejoice and be glad, O righteous elder Simeon,
For you accepted to carry in your arms the Redeemer of
*   our souls,*
Who grants us the Resurrection.

TROPARION OF THE FEAST

The Greek word *hypapante*, translated as the "meeting" or "encounter" of the Lord, is the name of a feast celebrated forty days after Christmas, thus bringing to a fitting conclusion the Advent/Christmas/Theophany cycle. This glorious feast, one of the most ancient ones in the Christian calendar, has been celebrated with great solemnity in the East from time immemorial. Many are the Fathers who wrote splendid sermons on the occasion of the feast: Methodious of Patara, Cyril of Jerusalem, Gregory the Theologian, Gregory of Nyssa, and John Chrysostom, among others. The feast, as many other feasts of the Lord and his holy Mother, originated in the East and from there it found its way much later to the

Christian West. There are vestiges of its eastern origins in some of the western liturgical texts for the feast.

The theme of the feast, "The Meeting of the Lord," commemorates the important event related in Luke 2: 22–40, that is, the Presentation of the Lord in the Jerusalem temple. According to custom and tradition, forty days after his birth, the Infant Jesus was taken by his parents to be presented to God in the temple. The temple was the pivotal center of religious life for all of Israel. It was the custom then, according to the law of Moses, for a woman who gave birth to a male child to be prohibited from entering the temple for a period of forty days. When the forty days were completed, the mother could then bring the child into the temple and offer him to the Lord, and at the same time bring a lamb or pigeons to serve as sacrificial offerings. Our Lady, the most holy *Theotokos*, did not fit this category since she was chosen to be the Mother of God; however, in her utter humility and devotion, she chose freely to fulfill this requisite of Israel's law. She, Saint Joseph, and the Baby Jesus made their pilgrimage to the temple just like any other ordinary Jewish family. By God's eternal design, an elder righteous man called Simeon was still living in Jerusalem at that time, as was the prophetess Anna. The Lord had revealed to Simeon that he would not face death until he beheld with his own eyes the Messiah, the Anointed One from above. The Gospel story tells us that Simeon arrived at the temple at the very moment Jesus' parents brought him in to fulfill the law. The texts of the Byzantine vespers relate beautifully the moment of this blessed encounter:

> *Simeon, tell us whom do you bear in your arms*
> *That you rejoice so greatly in the Temple?*

To whom do you cry out: Now I am set free
for I have seen my Savior?
This is he who was born of a Virgin,
This is he, the Word, God of God,
Who for our sakes has taken flesh and saved human-
    kind,
O come let us adore him!

Receive, O Simeon, him whom Moses beheld in the
    darkness of Sinai,
This is he who spoke through the Law,
This is he whose voice was heard by the prophets,
Who for our sakes has taken flesh and saved man-
    kind,
O come let us adore him.

The Gospel story relates that upon seeing the child, the blessed elder took him into his arms, thus becoming a *theodochos*, that is, a God-receiver. Embracing the child with his old, tired arms the elder began thanking the Lord, in the words we monks sing every night at Compline: "Now, Lord, you can let your servant go in peace, according to your word. For mine eyes have seen your salvation, which You have prepared in the face of every people. A light to enlighten the nations, and the glory of your people Israel." The Gospel tells that both Mary and Joseph were astonished at what was being said about the child. And as Simeon turned to bless them, he said to Mary, the child's mother, "This child is destined for the fall and rise of many in Israel, and to be a sign that will be contradicted (and you yourself a sword will pierce) so that the thoughts of many hearts may be revealed." And a Byzantine liturgical text adds: "O Pure Virgin! That which was fulfilled in you is beyond the understanding of angels and mortal men!" For how could the human mind comprehend what must have transpired at that very moment, in the heart of God's Mother, upon hearing Simeon's prophecy?

The icon of the feast shows another important person present at this blessed event. It is an old widow, the prophetess Anna, showing a scroll in her hands saying: "This child is the Lord of heaven and earth." Saint Luke in his Gospel tells us that Anna was the daughter of Phanuel of the tribe of Asher. She was long in years, having lived seventy years with her husband after her marriage. As a widow, at the age of eighty-four, she retired to live in the temple serving the Lord with prayer and fasting day and night. She also came into the temple at the very hour Simeon arrived and, upon seeing the child and his parents, began to praise God and continued to speak about the child to all those who were looking for the redemption of Jerusalem. An old Byzantine liturgical text sings her praises this way:

Holy Anna, sober in spirit and venerable in years,
Reverently received her master freely and openly in the temple,
And she proclaimed Mary to be the *Theotochos*,
Praising her in the presence of all the people.

Both Anna and elder Simeon lived holy lives, patiently waiting to see the Lord's day. They believed in the promise God had made to his people. They prayed day and night in the temple, thus remaining faithful to the Jewish tradition of constant prayer. They added fasting to their worship and lived with great humility among the worshippers. When their end was near, God saw fit to reward their efforts and fidelity by allowing them to behold with their very eyes the one who was to be the consolation and

Savior of Israel. They recognized him instantly, the moment his parents brought him into the temple. Simeon, filled with the spirit of the just and joy of the saints, bent down and reverently touched the footprints of the Mother of God, addressing her and saying: "O Most Pure Lady, he who you carry is fire. I am afraid to take God as a babe in my arms. He is the Lord of the light that knows no shadow..."(Byzantine Matins of the Feast).

Translations of Latin sentences that are at or near the end of some of the reflections

November 16 *Iucundare, filia Sion, exsulta satis, filia Jerusalem*: Rejoice greatly, O daughter of Sion, shout for joy, O daughter of Jerusalem.

November 17 *Veni, Sancte Spiritus*: Come, Holy Spirit.

November 18 *Ecce, Salvator venit*: Behold, the Savior came.

November 20 *Veni, Domine, visitare nos in pace*: Come, O Lord, visit us in peace.

November 23 *Veni, Emmanuel!* Come, Savior of all!

November 30 *Deo gratias!* Thanks be to God!

December 2	*Veni, Sancte Spiritus*: Come, Holy Spirit.
December 7	*Ecce, ego venio et habitabo in medio tui*: Behold I come, and I will dwell in the midst of thee.
December 9	*Iuste et pie vivamus, expectantes beatam spem et adventum Domini*: Justly and devoutly in this age, we await the blessed hope, the appearance of the glory of the great God.
December 10	*Veni Domine, et noli tardare*: Come Lord, and delay not.
December 15	*Gaude et laetare semper in Domino, filia Sion*: Rejoice and be glad always in the Lord, daughter of Sion.
December 16	*Ecce iam venit, plenitudo temporis, in quo misit Deus filium suum in terras*: Behold, now comes the fulfillment of time when God sends his Son to earth.
December 17	*Veni, ad docendum nos viam prudentiae*: Come, teach us the path of prudence [knowledge].
December 18	*Veni ad redimendum nos in brachio extento*: Come and with an outstretched arm redeem us.
December 21	*Veni et illumina sedentes in tenebris*: Come and enlighten those who sit in darkness.
December 22	*Veni, salva hominem, quem de limo formasti*: Come and save mankind, whom you shaped from the mud.
December 23	*Veni ad salvandum nos, Domine Deus noster*: Come save us, O Lord our God.